Richard L. Dresselhaus

The JOY of Belonging

A STUDY IN CHURCH MEMBERSHIP

RadiantBOOKS
Gospel Publishing House/Springfield, Mo. 65802

02-0526

Contents

Part 1: Your New Life in Christ

1 Welcome to the Family 6
2 Your Place in the Family 13
3 What Is Church Membership? 19
4 Your Walk With Christ 25

Part 2: Your Christian Growth

5 Keep on Growing 30
6 Following the Lord in Water Baptism . . . 37
7 A Personal Pentecost 42
8 Your Devotional Life 49

Part 3: Your Church and Its Structure

9 Foundations on Which to Build 54
10 The Structure of the Local Church 61

Part 4: Your Church and Its Mission

11 Upward in Worship 74
12 Inward in Commitment 86
13 Outward in Evangelism 91

Part 5: Your Church Membership Opportunities

14 Principles for Christian Service 96
15 Gifts for Service 101

Part 6: Your Home and Its Christian Influence

16 The Family and the Church 114

Appendix

Statement of Fundamental Truths 124

Part 1
Your New Life in Christ

1 Welcome to the Family

The church is people!

People just like you. People who have met the Lord . . . whose lives have been turned around . . . who love and want to be loved. People who are led together to become the people of God.

And this is where the story of the church begins—with you, for you are His church.

And that's what this book is about. People learning to live together as a community of believers . . . sharing, serving, giving, teaching, correcting, helping, and growing . . . until more and more we all become one in Jesus Christ.

So welcome. We are all glad you want to be a part of the family—the church.

Naturally you have a lot of questions:

"What are my responsibilities now that I have become a Christian?"

"How can I really grow in my walk with Christ and in my place of ministry in the church?"

"How is the church organized to carry on its mission, and what is my place in furthering that mission?"

"What are the doctrines of the church?"

"Why is it important that I become a member of a church?"

"What do I need to know to help me be an effective member of the church?"

I know you have dozens of other questions. But in these pages you will find the kind of answers that I hope will not only satisfy your curiosity but also motivate you to become dynamically and creatively involved in the exciting life of the church.

Let's start at the beginning. Do you remember when you first believed? It may have been at the altar bench or by your bedside late at night, or perhaps you don't remember the time and place—but you know it happened. Christ became Lord of your life, and you became a new creation.

The Bible uses a variety of words and expressions to describe this turning point in your life. Each speaks of action—newness, change, transformation, and hope. Let's look at them.

Born Again

Jesus used this descriptive term. "Nicodemus, you must be born again!"

Appropriately, Nicodemus countered: "Can a man enter his mother's womb and be born again?"

Jesus alleviated his suspicions: "That which is born of the flesh is flesh; and that which is born of the Spirit is spirit" (John 3:6).

Jesus instructed Nicodemus to submit to the power of the Holy Spirit so his spirit would be quickened and that communion with God, lost for so long, might be restored again.

The term *born again* describes this process. Once-dead men—dead in trespasses and sins—are now made alive in Jesus Christ.

This is God's way to bring you into His family. You

7

can't get in by argument, influence, or good conduct; it is a matter of birth. You have to be born into the family—the family of God.

Justification

This is another word to help you understand that turning point in your life. Paul used this term to describe how God looks at you now that you have been born again. The word has judicial overtones and really means "acquitted." The judge having ruled, the accused is declared innocent of the charge.

You stood guilty before a holy and righteous God. You had no other plea. But God, in His love and grace, declared you innocent.

How can that be? Someone must pay the penalty!

That is exactly what Jesus did. He satisfied the righteous demands of a perfect God and made it possible for God to declare you justified—innocent of the offense for which you stood guilty.

I once spoke at length with a young man who was having difficulty understanding that he now stood perfect, in Christ, before the Father. He had the mistaken notion that sometime, somehow, he could attain a place where eventually he could believe he was totally accepted by God.

Perhaps it is the miscarriage of this fundamental truth that brings relentless condemnation and fear to so many. The simple truth is because you have believed in Christ, you now stand before God totally accepted and justified. This is the place of rest you have been promised!

Salvation

This word also is highly suggestive. It is a word of

drama. It speaks of a man who has lost his way, or whose life was in peril, being rescued and freed.

How fitting that the very name *Jesus* means "Saviour." No wonder the angel of the Lord declared to Joseph, "You shall call His name Jesus, for it is He who will save His people from their sins" (Matthew 1:21).

Where would you be at this moment without Jesus the Saviour? How would you answer for your life if you knew you could not stand fully clothed in the righteous garments of Christ? Think of the vicious, destructive, debilitating effects of sin. That will help you know how really good it is to be "saved."

Atonement

The Israelites must have had a very good understanding of the meaning of this word. They even had one day a year set aside to celebrate the act of God's forgiveness in pardoning their sins—they called it the Day of Atonement. In elaborate and ceremonial fashion, the high priest presented the corporate sins of Israel to God, and God extended His forgiveness. The visible glory of God in the Holy of Holies signified His pardon.

The apostle Paul, against this background, spoke of Jesus: "Through whom we have now received the reconciliation [atonement]" (Romans 5:11). The word speaks of "fellowship restored," an "at oneness" with God. And Jesus Christ is the linchpin. By His vicarious death He has taken the hand of God and the hand of man and clasped them together. Every time a person comes to Christ, it is a beautiful return to that original relationship of love and fellowship. The ideal fellowship of the Garden of Eden becomes a reality again.

Forgiveness

A bumper sticker puts it this way: "Christians are not perfect, just forgiven." Christians have no claim to perfection, only a deep joy at knowing they are forgiven.

The ability to forgive is fundamental to the character of God. The Scriptures state that God not only forgives, He also forgets. That is, God possesses both the ability to say, "I forgive you," and the power to erase even the knowledge of the offense from His mind.

True forgiveness among men must be patterned after this. It is doubtful that forgiveness that is conditional or carries a lingering grudge can be considered forgiveness at all. "I forgive you, but I'll never forget," says something about the shallowness with which some people seek to alleviate their responsibility to forgive.

Yes, you have been forgiven.

When you were dead in your transgressions and the uncircumcision of your flesh, He made you alive together with Him, having forgiven us all our transgressions, having cancelled out the certificate of debt consisting of decrees against us and which was hostile to us; and He has taken it out of the way, having nailed it to the cross (Colossians 2:13, 14).

Your life bears the stamp of His forgiveness. The guilt is gone. Sin's hold has been broken. You are free!

Faith

A helpful formula has been suggested:

FAITH + 0 = SALVATION

This means a simple act of faith alone brings salvation. Paul put it this way: "For by grace you have been saved through faith; and that not of yourselves, it is a gift of God; not as a result of works, that no one should boast" (Ephesians 2:8, 9).

Sometimes this fundamental truth is misunderstood. Man innately wants to find a way to save himself. The notion of simple faith is an offense to his intellect. He wants to help himself—to find a way to earn merit with God. For him the formula reads: Faith plus good works, or faith plus knowledge, or faith plus a new revelation, or faith plus some other human ingredient.

Several years ago I visited the cathedral in Bath, England. I was deeply impressed with the elaborate structure. Two ladders were engraved in the stone on either side of the main entrance. On each ladder were likenesses of humans on their way up. Some were struggling upward, others had fallen, but none appeared to have reached the top. At the head of both ladders a figure, intended to represent the Lord, waited to welcome any successful climbers.

The imagery was intended to show man in his upward journey to find God and earn his salvation. While the architecture and design were aesthetically pleasing, the misunderstanding of God's plan to save man by simple faith in Jesus Christ was glaring and dramatic. God's way to himself is through faith in the finished work of Christ—alone!

Conversion

Conversion means the act of turning from one way to another. *Repentance* is a near synonym, with the same idea—that of turning around and heading in a different direction, a change of mind and heart.

The Bible illustrates this principle repeatedly. Most striking of all is the conversion of Saul, who later became the apostle Paul. The turning point came on the Damascus Road. In a moment of time Saul believed and reversed the direction of his life. He did an about-face. His life was completely altered; he had become a new creature in Jesus Christ.

This brief survey of terms and experiences will help you have a better understanding of the turning point in your life that brought you into the family of God. Whether or not you can identify the time and the place is not so important. What is important is the deep knowledge that you have passed from death unto life. This is where the journey begins!

2 Your Place in the Family

It is one thing to be saved; it is another to take your place in the body of Christ. The first has to do with a vertical relationship (you and God). The other has to do with horizontal relationships (you and everyone else).

God's call involves both. You can't have the one without the other. "If we walk in the light as He Himself is in the light, we have fellowship with one another, and the blood of Jesus His Son cleanses us from all sin" (1 John 1:7). Fellowship with God leads to fellowship with the people of God.

In fact, John went so far as to say: "The one who says he is in the light and yet hates his brother is in the darkness until now . . . and does not know where he is going because the darkness has blinded his eyes" (1 John 2:9, 11).

The point is clear. You are called into a new relationship with God in conversion, and you are also called into a new relationship with the body of Christ, the Church. Neither is optional.

What is the Church? We use the term in several ways.

It is not just a building, although we may speak of a church that is located at a certain address.

It is not just a denomination, although we may speak of "our church" and by that mean a particular denomination.

It is not just a corporation, although the laws of the land dictate a corporate structure.

It is not just an audience, although people are asked to listen to the proclamation of the Word.

It is not just a social center, although people find the church a pleasant place to gather with friends.

It is not just an entertainment center, although people will feel good about being there.

It is not just an educational institution, although the Word of God will be faithfully taught there.

What then is the Church?

The Church Is a Body

The apostle Paul used the human body as a metaphor to describe this function:

For even as the body is one and yet has many members, and all the members of the body, though they are many, are one body, so also is Christ. . . . But now God has placed the members, each one of them, in the body, just as He desired (1 Corinthians 12:12, 18).

Continuing, Paul spoke specifically of some of the varied functions of the individual members of the Body: "God has appointed in the church, first apostles, second prophets, third teachers, then miracles, then gifts of healings, helps, administrations, various kinds of tongues" (1 Corinthians 12:28).

This list is continued in Romans:

Since we have gifts that differ according to the grace given to us, let each exercise them accordingly: if prophecy, according to the proportion of his faith; if service, in his serving; or he who teaches, in his teaching; or he who exhorts, in his exhortation; he who gives, with liberality; he who leads, with diligence; he who shows mercy, with cheerfulness (Romans 12:6-8).

14

You are a member of this Body. You are tempered together with the other members to make His body complete. You have spiritual gifts and enablements that will make you a vital part of the Body. You will now be encouraged to identify those gifts and enablements and cultivate them into fruitful service. Your service to Christ through His body will be on this basis. You will need to do what the Holy Spirit has equipped you to do.

The Church Is an Organism

The Church is not static; it is dynamic. Within, it has a life principle that gives it reproductive power. When the Church is healthy, it will reproduce itself over and over again. Extinction occurs only when an organism is weakened from within and is no longer able to reproduce itself.

Much is said these days about evangelism. And as a member of the Church you will share that concern. But be sure you keep perspective. There are many worthwhile programs of outreach, but none will be fruitful unless the body maintains its spiritual health. When it does, evangelism is inevitable. A spiritual, dynamic, and alive church will attract to itself those who see its quality of life as authentic and real.

A contemporary theologian has properly asserted that the church must be the showpiece of Christianity to the world. This is what makes the church grow and flourish. It stands up to its generation and visibly and openly demonstrates the transforming power of Jesus Christ. It is to this challenge you are called.

The Church Is a "Community"

God has called His people to live and serve together.

Paul addressed Epistles to the church in Rome, Ephesus, Colossae, Philippi, and other major cities of his day. The Church universal is called to identify itself locally as the community of believers in that place. In this sense the local church is merely the localization of the universal Church. Or, in other words, it is the invisible Church made visible. As such, it may appropriately be referred to as a community.

Luke the historian describes that early community of believers in Jerusalem:

Those who had received his word were baptized; and there were added that day about three thousand souls. And they were continually devoting themselves to the apostles' teaching and to fellowship, to the breaking of bread and to prayer. . . . And day by day continuing with one mind in the temple, and breaking bread from house to house, they were taking their meals together with gladness and sincerity of heart (Acts 2:41, 42, 46).

The church in Jerusalem was visible, communal, and local.

The apostle Paul set out to establish communities of believers in the major population centers of the ancient world. The pattern is clear:

And the next day he went away with Barnabas to Derbe. And after they had preached the gospel to that city and had made many disciples, they returned to Lystra and to Iconium and to Antioch, strengthening the souls of the disciples, encouraging them to continue in the faith. . . . And when they had appointed elders for them in every church, having prayed with fasting, they commended them to the Lord in whom they had believed (Acts 14:20-23).

In this way many local churches were established.

You have been called to be a part of a community.

16

You have been called out of the world to be a part of the people of God. This will mean a total commitment on your part. You cannot live in this community and not give yourself to it. Implicit in the call is a challenge to yield up everything for the work and service of Christ. Secret discipleship is not acceptable; you must declare yourself to be part of the church, the community of God's people.

The Church Is a Fellowship

Luke the historian reports that believers in the first church ". . . were continually devoting themselves to the apostles' teaching and to fellowship *[koinonia]*, to the breaking of bread and to prayer" (Acts 2:42). Theirs was an open, honest, and transparent sharing of their lives. The Greek word *koinonia* speaks of giving and sharing. It carries the idea of giving away your life to another—or of letting others into the inner circle of your life.

By nature man is prone to hide. In the Garden of Eden man was free to share his life with God—to be open, honest, and transparent. But with the entrance of sin man became aware of his nakedness and sought to hide from God. From that moment to this God has been calling: "Where are you?" And man has been answering: "I was afraid because I was naked; so I hid myself" (Genesis 3:9, 10).

It is most interesting to observe that prior to the Fall Adam and Eve were naked, yet were not ashamed. But sin changed that.

Man from that time until this has attempted in a multitude of ways to hide from himself, from others, and from God. It may take the form of isolationism, anger, hostility, feelings of inferiority, or insecurity. Each is a

17

shield behind which man may hide from who he really is.

In the body of Christ you do not need to hide. You can be free to be yourself—a new creature in Jesus Christ. Free to be open with God and with others. There is no longer cause for hiding. Christ died on the cross that you might not need to hide any longer. It is safe to come out. His blood has made you whole.

The church is the place to enjoy this new freedom. It is a life of openness and freedom—honesty and acceptance. So much so that James could confidently say: "Confess your sins to one another, and pray for one another, so that you may be healed" (James 5:16). Or as Paul put it: "Bear one another's burdens, and thus fulfill the law of Christ" (Galatians 6:2).

All of us have observed, with sad regret, believers who have been content to frequent the worship services of the local church, share in its activities, yet never experience its inner life. Tragic, but true.

People build about them an impregnable wall. They live in isolation, refusing to share in the inner life that unites believers and makes them one in the body of Christ. This has to be one of the greatest of all contradictions. Perhaps they have never understood the Church provides the occasion for everyone to come out from hiding and be free. Why? Because they have failed to understand that Jesus took all of our shame and put it on the cross.

So you are part of a life-sharing Fellowship—members together in the body of Christ.

3 What Is Church Membership?

The four definitions of the Church described in the preceding chapter relate primarily to what we sometimes call the invisible Church or the Church universal. Membership in this Church is automatic. We believe every person who is born again becomes a member of that Church at the time of his or her salvation experience.

There are no membership cards to fill out—as such. Your acceptance of Christ as Saviour and Lord—your commitment of your life to Him—means you are a member of His church, born into the family of God.

But now you are being asked to join a local church—a visible division of that invisible Body. It will involve another decision on your part—a commitment to identify with a group of believers who worship and serve together.

Here are some questions you may have about that decision.

If I Am Already a Member of the Church Through Faith in Christ, Why Is It Necessary for Me to Become a Member of a Local Church?

We believe local church membership will affect your spiritual progress in a dramatic way. That is why so much of this book deals with the matter of Christian growth and maturity.

Why Must the Local Church Have a Formal Membership?

That too is a valid question. In fact, some churches don't. While there may appear to be merit to this approach, I feel believers are being cheated out of opportunities to grow if they are not challenged to become a committed part of a local fellowship of believers. I think they should publicly declare their willingness to accept both the privileges and the responsibilities of affiliation with a local body of believers. The world needs to know where we stand and how we understand our place in the church.

Does the Bible Say I Must Be a Member of a Local Church?

No, not in so many words. But it certainly does speak of commitment. And that should be the emphasis of church membership. The signing of a membership card can hardly be meaningful in itself—but the act of commitment which it represents is of great importance.

The Early Church did not lose sight of individual commitment and identity. Luke reports, "The Lord was adding to their number day by day those who were being saved" (Acts 2:47).

Can I Have Ministry in the Church Without Formally Becoming a Member?

Every church has its own set of qualifications for ministry. In some cases membership is requested prior to an appointment for ministry. In other churches that provision is not required. It seems best to me that individuals be chosen for leadership positions when they have demonstrated their commitment to the church through church membership.

What Are the Requirements to Become a Member of the Local Church?

Here too the requirements for church membership vary from church to church. These very general qualifications likely will be embodied in the statement of requirements in most Assemblies of God churches:

a. Clear evidence of a genuine experience of regeneration (John 1:12, 13; 3:3-8; 1 Peter 1:18-25).

b. Discernible evidence of a consistent Christian life (Romans 6:4; 13:13, 14; Ephesians 4:17-32; 5:1, 2, 15; 1 John 1:6, 7).

c. Baptism in water (Matthew 28:19; Mark 16:16; Romans 6:3-5).

d. Baptism in the Holy Spirit (Acts 2:4) or a diligent seeking for the baptism in the Holy Spirit (Luke 24:49; Acts 1:4).

e. A willingness to subscribe to the Statement of Fundamental Truths as set forth by the Assemblies of God.

f. A willingness to assume the responsibilities of stewardship through faithfulness in attendance, in serving, and in giving (Proverbs 3:9; 1 Corinthians 4:2; Hebrews 10:25).

Are There Different Types of Church Membership?

Yes. Usually Assemblies of God churches offer three types of church membership or some variation of them:

a. *Adult membership.* This includes all who meet the requirements set forth above and who meet the age requirements outlined in the constitution and bylaws of any given church. In most cases the minimum age for church membership is between 16 and 18 years of age.

b. *Associate membership.* This includes those who meet the requirements as stated above yet are not listed as "adult members." College students in residence in a city other than home, young people not yet having reached the minimum age, military personnel stationed away from home, and others who may be temporarily living in another community all find themselves in this membership category. Associate members are not granted the privilege of voting, nor may they be elected to any official position.

c. *Junior membership.* It is important that families join the church as units. Even children need to know they belong. Junior membership provides this opportunity. Included here are children who have been born again yet are not old enough to qualify for associate membership. The age boundaries for associate and junior membership are established in the constitution and bylaws of the individual church.

What Are My Financial Responsibilities as a Member of the Church?

This subject will be treated again in a later chapter. Perhaps it is adequate here to point out the Scriptures teach that every believer is to give a tithe (a tenth) of his income to the work of the Lord. Besides this, he will want to give offerings as the Lord prospers him.

Some object that tithing is an Old Testament concept and the New Testament does not reaffirm it. Here is a brief answer to this objection:

a. The principle of the tithe is not limited to any particular period of history. Abraham offered a tithe to

Melchizedek several hundred years before the Law was given. In the New Testament Jesus rebuked the Pharisees for omitting the weightier matters of the Law, but commended them for tithing.

Although the New Testament does not specifically require the tithe, it does assume its existence as a common practice among the pious.

b. In the New Testament the believer is introduced to a higher level of stewardship based on God's grace. The believer, living under grace, recognizes everything he has was given him by God and rightfully belongs to God. He now has the privilege of giving out of a heart of love in joyful response to God's manifest grace in his life.

c. It is a contradiction to suppose believers living under grace should give less than those believers who lived under the Law. The fundamental difference lies in the area of motivation. Under the Law giving was a duty and a requirement. Under grace giving is a privilege and an opportunity. The one says, "You must"; the other says, "I want to."

Giving to God is a great joy. It provides a tangible way to cooperate with God. It builds character and inspires faith. It is one of God's ways to bring His children into a relationship of trust. You too will find great blessing through faithfulness in stewardship.

* * * * *

The preceding questions are typical of those most often asked about church membership. The fundamental issue is still the matter of commitment. Each believer must come to grips with his need to identify with a local church. He must be willing to publicly declare himself. He must be willing to say: "This is my church—it is where I belong."

23

That commitment will provide the setting for dramatic spiritual growth in the believer's life and will speak loudly to the world about the importance of the church and the direction of its mission.

People who feel they would rather remain unattached fail to grasp the true significance of the church. The church is comprised of a committed people—people who have covenanted together to be the people of God in a given locale.

It is a gross contradiction to imagine the body of Christ can function without commitment from its members. Be glad you have been led of the Holy Spirit to become a member of the local church. It is God's way for you to grow and to bear His witness in your world.

4 Your Walk With Christ

The question of Christian conduct must be a part of any serious discussion of church membership. It is appropriate that you ask: "How am I expected to live as a member of the church? Are there rules of conduct? Are there certain activities from which I should abstain? What are the standards of the church?"

The criteria by which Christian conduct is measured will vary from church to church and from one geographical area to another—to say nothing about cross-cultural variables and influences. So I will simply set forth fundamental Biblical principles that relate to Christian conduct and then allow the application of these principles to serve as a guide for acceptable Christian conduct.

The Bible Is the Rule Book
for Christian Conduct

When a church does speak, it must find its authority in the letter and the spirit of the Scriptures. Appropriately, the first church council which convened in Jerusalem around A.D. 50 expressed a concern that the churches not be placed under unbearable and unattainable demands and requirements: "For it seemed good to the Holy Spirit and to us to lay upon you no greater burden than these essentials" (Acts 15:28).

The Scriptures provide an adequate set of guidelines in the way of purity and spiritual maturity. It is impossible to find any aspect of contemporary life that is not addressed in the Scriptures—if not in letter, certainly in spirit.

No church that has had its anchor in the Word has ever suffered a moral and spiritual decline. The Psalmist clearly understood this when he said: "Thy word I have treasured in my heart, that I may not sin against Thee" (Psalm 119:11).

Use the Scriptures as the rule book in all matters. When the directive comes from the Scriptures, it carries with it an authority and a power that will make it a reality in your life. Even prohibitions, that come from the Word produce life.

Right Conduct Demands Right Motivation

What is it in a person that makes for good behavior? Is true righteousness the product of external or internal forces? What is the fundamental problem when a believer's conduct becomes a reproach?

The apostle Paul spoke of his great desire for the Galatian believers that "Christ [be] formed" in them (Galatians 4:19). Over and over Paul spoke of the believer being in Christ and Christ being in the believer: "For you have died and your life is hidden with Christ in God" (Colossians 3:3). "Therefore if any man is in Christ, he is a new creature; the old things passed away; behold, new things have come" (2 Corinthians 5:17).

That says it all—the inner motivation for living the transformed and risen life is the dynamic of Jesus

Christ, whose life is being lived out from within the believer.

The World Will Measure the Church by Your Life

Paul said it unequivocally: "You are our letter, . . . known and read of all men" (2 Corinthians 3:2). Repeatedly Jesus spoke of love as the evidence of discipleship before the world. Yes, the world is watching; and it will measure the church by taking a reading on your life.

In your place as a member of the church your life will be continuously observed, and your conduct will either contribute to the impact of your church or detract from it. This is a responsibility you assume first as a believer and then as a member of a local church. You are part of the showpiece, and you have invited the world to look.

It is impossible to overemphasize the importance of a church's reputation in a community. You are part of that reputation. An unkempt house, a lawn that is grown up in weeds, a mailbox full of overdue bills, a curt response on the phone, a harsh word to a clerk, an unkind frown on the freeway, or whatever: these are the things that subtract from the reputation of your church.

Remember, when it comes to faith, seeing is believing. That is what the world believes, and they are the ones we want to win!

I will never forget a very minor incident at a city intersection in which my car was abruptly bumped from the back. It was more of an irritant than anything else. I was thankful I had held my feelings in check when the offender said: "Oh, you are the minister who conducted the funeral. I was there."

A little matter? Yes. Yet these are the everyday happenings in life that add to or subtract from the reputation of the church and the message it preaches. Treat every person you meet as an inquirer after Jesus Christ. You are being watched!

Part 2
Your Christian Growth

5 Keep on Growing

The name of the game is *change*.

That is what growth is all about. Moving from one level of spiritual comprehension to the next. Leaving old paths for new. Discovering what was once hidden. And seeing for the first time new answers to old questions. It is all part of growth.

A preacher was once asked, "What produces spiritual growth?"

He replied, "Conflict."

And really he was right. It is not until we are caught in a rub that we realize how tender our feelings are. It is not until we are crossed that we discover how self-centered and willful we tend to be. It takes people at our elbows to help us to see ourselves for what we really are.

The coach would not think of trying to "finish" a team without subjecting that team to scrimmage. When the team is on the field and in the tensions of competition, weaknesses are exposed and strengths revealed.

The same is true in the church. People from all walks of life, from every conceivable economic and social strata and from every personality type imaginable, are put together in one place to become the people of God. At first they don't all fit. But after a while the rough edges are cut away, and a beautiful new Christian emerges. Growth comes through conflict.

Here are some principles of Christian growth.

The Way of Servitude

Jesus said: "The Son of Man did not come to be served, but to serve, and to give His life a ransom for many" (Matthew 20:28). This is an important step on the journey to spiritual maturity.

This is not an easy principle to follow. On the surface it gains immediate acceptance—but wait until the test comes!

"Why didn't I get the credit? I did the work!"

"It seems like I'm always the one who gets asked to do everything."

"I wish someone would think of me—at least just once."

It is a dead giveaway. A servant's heart has not yet been developed. The urge is to seek for position, for recognition, for acclaim. It is human and natural—but wrong!

This is what Jesus asks us to forsake. The call of the Master is to service. And that call cuts across the fabric of our humanity.

What a relief when once we learn the joy of humble service. This is what Jesus taught: "He who has found his life shall lose it, and he who has lost his life for My sake shall find it" (Matthew 10:39). "If any one wants to be first, he shall be last of all, and servant of all" (Mark 9:35). "I say to you, unless a grain of wheat falls into the earth and dies, it remains by itself alone; but if it dies, it bears much fruit" (John 12:24).

The truth is plain. The believer is asked to take up his cross and follow Christ. From that moment on he is no longer his own. He is a love-slave to Christ and servant to all who are His.

Walking in the Light

This principle is suggested in 1 John 1:7: "If we walk in the light as He Himself is in the light, we have fellowship with one another, and the blood of Jesus His Son cleanses us from all sin." In other words, the criterion for fellowship is living in openness and transparency as members of the body of Chirst. It is a willingness to come to grips with our sins so we may walk together in the purity of His light.

The same note was struck by James: "Confess your sins to one another, and pray for one another, so that you may be healed" (James 5:16). James here equates physical health with "relationship health." We have all seen how that works itself out. Bitterness, animosity, hatred, and variance are poisonous. Given time, these negative attributes will ruin a person mentally, physically, and spiritually.

Jesus said: "I am the way, and the truth, and the life" (John 14:6). In another place He declared: "You shall know the truth, and the truth shall make you free" (John 8:32). Believers may experience inner freedom through the dynamic of truth at work in their lives.

One of the most powerful prayers I know is this: "Lord, allow the spirit of truth to prevail."

In answer to that prayer the Holy Spirit is able to expose lies, reveal impure motives, and bring deep inner healing. I have seen it happen over and over again. And remember the Holy Spirit has a continuing ministry. He not only reveals truth and exposes error, He also is faithful to impart the very life of Jesus. This is the key to positive Christian growth and maturity.

Understanding Authority

The fundamental question of the universe is the question of authority. Satan quizzed our first parents: "Hath God said?" And even long before that Lucifer attempted to rob God of His deity. In both instances it was a clear question of authority: who would rule and who would be ruled?

A child learns early in life to resist authority—in fact, it just comes naturally. His retort, "No, I will not!" is evidence enough.

The human race is shot through with rebellion. We have an authority crisis in our world. Children set against parents, nation against nation, race against race, brother against brother—it all boils down to a fundamental question of authority.

The church too is caught in this tension. Who has the authority? Who has the right to make decisions? Who is to lead, and who is to follow?

Sooner or later you will find yourself in the middle of this question. How you deal with it will measure your Christian maturity.

So-called "church problems" are invariably caused by a confusion over authority.

God has set certain authorities over you for your good. How you regard these authorities will determine to a large degree your rate of spiritual growth.

Take your place in the church. Recognize those whom God has placed over you for your good. Be supportive and open. Don't resist their counsel. Pray for them—that they may have the wisdom of the Lord. And if you do, you will find a place of joy and service that will fulfill your highest expectation.

The Way of Relinquishment

The best example of relinquishment is the Cross: "For you know the grace of our Lord Jesus Christ, that though He was rich, yet for your sake He became poor, that you through His poverty might become rich" (2 Corinthians 8:9). The divestment of Jesus is seen too in the words of Paul: "Although He existed in the form of God, [He] did not regard equality with God a thing to be grasped, but emptied Himself, taking the form of a bondservant" (Philippians 2:6, 7).

Jesus laid aside His rights. He totally disregarded His rightful prerogatives as God. He emptied himself—became a servant—and died a criminal's death.

He is the model. You are asked to take up your cross and follow Him. Your personal rights must yield. You are no longer your own. Your life belongs to another.

What will further the work of the Lord? What is the best way to get the job done? What can I do to help a brother be more effective in his service for Christ? These become the big questions now. The effectiveness of your service to Christ will be in proportion to your willingness to lay aside your own personal rights and seek only those that are His.

The Ministry of Brokenness

There are scores of illustrations. The alabaster box was broken so the fragrance of its contents could be released. The grape must be pressed before it will yield its sweetness. The corn of wheat must be buried before it can release its life. Christ, the Son of God, had to die so His redemptive love could flow to man.

It is a principle with God—only through brokenness can true beauty be seen.

The Psalmist expressed it this way: "The sacrifices of God are a broken spirit; a broken and a contrite heart, O God, Thou wilt not despise" (Psalm 51:17).

Paul in his second letter to the Corinthians said: "If

we are afflicted, it is for your comfort and salvation; or if we are comforted, it is for your comfort, which is effective in the patient enduring of the same sufferings which we also suffer" (1:6). In the next chapter Paul added: "But thanks be to God, who always leads us in His triumph in Christ, and manifests through us the sweet aroma of the knowledge of Him in every place" (2:14).

You are not expected to be a superstar in the body of Christ. You are asked only to serve the Lord with an attitude and spirit of brokenness. Even your weaknesses and failures will be turned to triumph. What you have viewed as ashes the Lord will use as materials with which to build His kingdom.

Caution! Brokenness of spirit and contrition of heart do not mean weakness. The most humble and broken will be the strongest—for they stand not in their own strength but in His. This is the clear teaching of the Word. Jesus was a humble, gentle, and broken Man. Yet even on the cross He demonstrated a strength and power no man could ever equal. In His moment of seeming weakness, He defeated the powers of darkness and won for man a place again with the Father.

Unilateral Forgiveness

Here is a principle of spiritual growth that will bring you spiritual power and blessing in your relationships with the members of the body of Christ.

When Jesus was about to die on the cross, He uttered these words: "Father forgive them; for they do not know what they are doing" (Luke 23:24). He did not wait until the Roman soldiers demonstrated a repentant spirit; He simply forgave them—unilaterally.

Unilateral forgiveness has to do with our forgiving a

brother even before he asks to be forgiven. This kind of forgiveness places on itself no conditions or restrictions—it simply extends forgiveness.

Let me illustrate: You have been falsely accused. The offending brother is unapproachable and confident he is right. You recognize that a corrective word will not now be received. Rather than become bitter and hostile, you forgive him in your spirit. The Holy Spirit can then minister through you to that brother and hopefully bring him to a place of repentance.

Judgmentalism is so often found in the church. It takes hold like a vise. It immobilizes the body of Christ. Jesus said: "Do not judge lest you be judged yourselves. For in the way you judge, you will be judged; and by your standard of measure, it shall be measured to you" (Matthew 7:1, 2).

Let forgiveness stand in the place of judgment. Dispense forgiveness.

There is an obvious reason why it is folly to judge a brother: You never possess all the facts! And this is the reason the Lord says: "Vengeance is mine. I will repay" (Romans 12:19). Only God possesses a total understanding. He alone is able to judge.

This principle will be invaluable as you live out your faith in the body of Christ. When offended, you will forgive. When hurt, you will love. When wronged, you will not judge. All of this will produce in you a free and victorious spirit.

All these principles for spiritual growth can best be summarized by these words: "Let Jesus stand between you and your world." Look at your brother through the eyes of Christ. Feel his hurt as Christ would feel it. Love him as you know Christ has loved him.

6 Following the Lord in Water Baptism

Water baptism is a vital part of spiritual growth. It stands as a monument in the believer's life. It is a clear point of reference—an anchor in time to mark a public confession of faith in Jesus Christ.

The Early Church recognized water baptism as the seal and proof of a commitment to Christ. Many believers paid with their lives for having submitted to water baptism.

The Example of Jesus

John understandably hesitated to comply with the request of Jesus for water baptism: "I have need to be baptized by You, and do You come to me?" Then Jesus explained: "Permit it at this time; for in this way it is fitting for us to fulfill all righteousness."

When Jesus came up out of the water John "saw the Spirit of God descending as a dove, and coming upon Him, and behold, a voice out of the heavens, saying, 'This is My beloved Son, in whom I am well-pleased' " (Matthew 3:14-17).

Why was it necessary for Jesus to be baptized? He said it was necessary for Him to fulfill all righteousness.

Paul gave a further explanation: "He made Him who knew no sin to be sin on our behalf, that we might become the righteousness of God in Him" (2 Corinthians 5:21).

The Incarnation demanded total identity with man—even with his sin. Only as the sin-bearer could He die for the sins of every man. The baptism of Jesus was necessitated by His servanthood. The suffering Servant "poured out Himself to death, and was numbered with the transgressors; yet He Himself bore the sin of many, and interceded for the transgressors" (Isaiah 53:12).

It is now the Lord who instructs us: "Go therefore and make disciples of all the nations, baptizing them in the name of the Father and the Son and the Holy Spirit" (Matthew 28:19).

We have both an example and a command. Water baptism is not optional. The Church is under mandate. And the privilege of compliance is ours.

The Meaning of Water Baptism

The meaning of water baptism is graphically portrayed in Paul's words to the believers in Rome:

Therefore we have been buried with Him through baptism into death, in order that as Christ was raised from the dead through the glory of the Father, so we too might walk in newness of life. For if we have become united with Him in the likeness of His death, certainly we shall be also in the likeness of His resurrection (Romans 6:4, 5).

The following statements will help to clarify the meaning of water baptism.

1. *It is an identification with Christ.* This is the pivotal truth. Water baptism is an identification with Jesus Christ in His death and His resurrection. The cross is lifted and the empty tomb visited in water baptism. It is as if time has lost its power to separate, and the be-

liever is made one with Christ on the cross and one with Christ in His triumphant resurrection.

2. *It is the pledge and testimony of a new life.* I like the words of the apostle Peter on this: "Baptism now saves you—not the removal of dirt from the flesh, but an appeal to God for a good conscience—through the resurrection of Jesus Christ" (1 Peter 3:21).

The word translated "appeal" could also be translated "demand." The point is clear. The act of water baptism does not in itself eradicate sin, but it does signal a changed heart. In baptism the believer pledges before men and before God that he will walk in obedience with Jesus Christ—his life has been transformed!

3. *It is an act of fellowship.* Paul put it this way: "There is one body and one Spirit, just as also you were called in one hope of your calling; one Lord, one faith, one baptism, one God and Father of all who is over all and through all and in all" (Ephesians 4:4-6). Water baptism is a celebration of the unity of the body of Christ.

Perhaps you have some questions.

"Why does the church believe in immersion?"

The word *baptize* means "to put under, or to immerse." Philip and the eunuch went *down into* the water together. Jesus himself was baptized by John in the Jordan River. The mode of baptism in both cases was obviously immersion. Baptism by immersion appropriately speaks of our identity with Christ in His death and resurrection.

"How old do you have to be to be baptized?"

The Scriptures place no age requirement for water baptism. The pattern, however, is first faith and then baptism. When a child has reached the age of spiritual comprehension and has clearly given testimony to a personal knowledge of Christ as Saviour, baptism in water should follow.

"What is the correct baptismal formula?"

In Matthew 28 Jesus spoke of baptism "in the name of the Father and the Son and the Holy Spirit" (v. 19). In Acts 2 Peter instructed the multitude: "Repent, and let each of you be baptized in the name of Jesus Christ for the forgiveness of your sins" (v. 38). The formula given by Jesus is the one usually followed. It speaks of the Trinity, reminiscent of the descending dove and the voice of God which spoke out of heaven at the baptism of Jesus.

"Should I be rebaptized?"

This question exists with believers who were sprinkled as babies, who have been baptized as adults without a clear knowledge of Christ as Lord and Saviour, or who have fallen out of fellowship with Christ and have now returned to a place of faith. The Scriptures are silent on the question. Yet if there is no memory of baptism or if baptism was without meaning, rebaptism would seem most appropriate.

"Is it necessary to be baptized in water to be saved?"

This is an inappropriate question. The question of the eunuch is the right question: "Look! Water! What prevents me from being baptized?" (Acts 8:36). In other words, what possible reason could there be for a believer to avoid water baptism?

Granted, the repentant thief was ushered into paradise without baptism, but that should hardly serve as a pattern. Aside from physical limitations or some other constraining circumstances, every believer should be baptized. Water baptism is a privilege of the highest order. Who would want to miss its joy?

You will need to understand the procedure for baptism. Too often candidates are distracted by some external factor that hinders concentration on the true meaning of baptism. Don't let that happen to you!

Allow the Holy Spirit to make water baptism a dynamic worship experience. Do not permit the ceremonial dimension to rob you of an encounter with Jesus Christ. Be free to respond to the presence of Christ with praise and worship.

View the baptismal service as an opportunity for evangelism. Your relatives and friends will likely come to your baptismal service. There may well be someone who will look back to that service as the spiritual turning point in his or her life.

Remember, water baptism is a gift of love to the Church. It is intended to be a source of special spiritual blessing. You can be sure Jesus Christ will manifest himself in wonderful ways through water baptism.

7   A Personal Pentecost

To speak of spiritual growth is to speak of the work of the Holy Spirit, for it is the prerogative of the Spirit to produce the likeness of Jesus in the believer's life.

Space is limited, but perhaps it will suffice to deal with some of the historical roots, the actual receiving of the baptism in the Holy Spirit, and then consider the fruit and gifts of the Spirit.

Historical Considerations

First, the Holy Spirit was active in the Old Testament. Repeatedly the Old Testament Scriptures speak of the dynamics of the Holy Spirit at work in the lives of great men of God. Several examples:

The Spirit of God came upon Balaam to prophesy (Numbers 24:2).

Othniel judged Israel under the direction of the Spirit of the Lord (Judges 3:10).

Gideon's great faith was motivated by the Spirit of the Lord that rested on him (Judges 6:34).

The supernatural strength of Samson is traceable to the Spirit's work in his life (Judges 14:6).

Saul was given to the ministry of prophecy as the Spirit directed him (1 Samuel 10:10).

The anointing of national leadership was by the

authority and direction of the Spirit (1 Samuel 16:13).

When we come to the New Testament, the same Spirit is active in creative, life-giving ways. When on the Day of Pentecost the Holy Spirit was outpoured, the place was shaken and they began to speak in languages previously unknown. And when Paul later spoke of the Scriptures as being inspired ("God-breathed"), we are not the least surprised. All of these beautifully demonstrate the life-giving, creative, energizing character and ministry of the Holy Spirit.

The Baptism in the Holy Spirit

Against this background we turn now to a discussion of what the Scriptures call being baptized with or in the Holy Spirit.

John the Baptist was the spokesman and Matthew the writer: "As for me, I baptize you in water for repentance, but He who is coming after me is mightier than I, and I am not even fit to remove His sandals; He Himself will baptize you with the Holy Spirit and fire" (Matthew 3:11).

Jesus left His disciples with this directive: "And behold, I am sending forth the promise of My Father upon you; but you are to stay in the city until you are clothed with power from on high" (Luke 24:49).

In Acts 2 that promise was fulfilled: "And they were all filled with the Holy Spirit and began to speak with other tongues, as the Spirit was giving them utterance" (v. 4).

A similar outpouring of the Spirit is recorded in Acts 10 in reference to the preaching of Peter in the house of Cornelius. "While Peter was still speaking these words, the Holy Spirit fell upon all those who were listening to the message. . . . They were hearing them speaking with tongues and exalting God" (vv. 44, 46).

Paul inquired of the Christians in Ephesus: "Did you receive the Holy Spirit when you believed?" Then following words of explanation, the narrative goes on: "And when Paul had laid his hands upon them, the Holy Spirit came on them, and they began speaking with tongues and prophesying" (Acts 19:2, 6).

The experience described in these passages is recurring with frequency in our day. The prophecy of Joel is being fulfilled (Joel 2:28, 29). You too may receive the gift of the Holy Spirit—the infilling or baptism in the Holy Spirit.

But how? Let me share with you some observations that may help you in receiving the Baptism.

It is a gift. Do not yield to the arguments of some who put the baptism in the Holy Spirit on the basis of merit. Somehow, they insist, the believer must meet certain qualifications. The only qualification I see in the Scriptures is a humble heart of faith. The Holy Spirit is the gift of the Father—available to all persons who simply believe.

It is not speaking in tongues. Speaking in tongues is a sign or evidence the Spirit has come. It is not the experience itself. When a believer is filled with the Spirit, the whole personality and character is affected. It is a good deal more than speaking in tongues.

It is not a proof of spirituality. The Pentecostal Movement has suffered unnecessarily at the hands of critics who have observed a self-righteousness among some Pentecostal believers. They have picked up on the "we-have-something-you-don't-have" attitude.

In reality, the baptism in the Holy Spirit is not a thermometer by which to measure spiritual status—it is a blessed gift of the Father to help us to be more like Jesus and to be effective in building His kingdom.

It is not received by constraint. Since the baptism in the Spirit is a gift, it is inappropriate, if not contradictory, to suppose the use of certain "techniques" will produce the Baptism. Jesus is the Baptizer. Fellow believers need only create an atmosphere of faith and expectancy. In that environment the Spirit is sure to be present.

It is a growing relationship. We have already seen the Holy Spirit, the "breath of God," is creative and dynamic. The baptism in the Holy Spirit is a relationship with the Spirit. As such, it is a growing and developing relationship. It is but the beginning of what Paul calls the Spirit-filled or Spirit-controlled life.

What matters most is that you respond affirmatively to what the Scriptures teach about being filled with the Spirit. If you have not yet received since you believed, why not do so now—by faith?

If you have already received, why not release yourself more fully to the creative and dynamic power of the Holy Spirit? You will find the Spirit-filled life will bring you into the likeness of Christ and empower you for effective service for Him.

Jesus said: "You shall receive power when the Holy Spirit has come upon you; and you shall be My witnesses both in Jerusalem, and in all Judea and Samaria, and even to the remotest part of the earth" (Acts 1:8).

The Fruit of the Spirit

Look at the fruit of the Spirit-filled life. Paul set it forth: "But the fruit of the Spirit is love, joy, peace, patience, kindness, goodness, faithfulness, gentleness, self-control" (Galatians 5:22, 23).

45

The fruit of the Spirit is the world's evidence of a Spirit-filled life. The people of the world are not interested in spiritual platitudes and opinions—they want to see the fruit. One act of kindness is worth a thousand words about the meaning of kindness. A demonstration of patience will be far more convincing than a discourse on the subject. A friend will be convinced of the necessity of self-control when you model that virtue in your own life. It is fruit the world craves—and rightly so.

Unfortunately some have put the gifts of the Spirit above the fruit of the Spirit. They revel in the ecstacy of religious experience to the exclusion of practical Christian living. The gifts of the Spirit have their validation in the fruit of the Spirit. The call in our day is for dynamic religious experience that finds its expression in the everyday affairs of living. Anything less than this is an insult to God!

The Lord will help you to be an example of a Spirit-filled and Spirit-controlled Christian. Ask Him to produce within you these very attributes that distinguish His own character.

The Gifts of the Spirit

In proper sequence we turn now to a consideration of the gifts of the Holy Spirit. The nine listed in 1 Corinthians 12:8-10 are included here with only a brief definition.

1. *The vocal gifts.* These three gifts have to do with verbal expressions that are spoken to glorify God and to build and edify the body of Christ.

a. Prophecy: The God-given ability to speak forth the thoughts of God for the correction, edification, and strengthening of the church.

b. Unknown tongues: The God-given ability to speak

forth in an unknown language the praises and exaltation of God.

c. Interpretation of tongues: The God-given ability to give the meaning of the unknown tongue so the whole church might be strengthened and built up.

2. *The power gifts.* These three gifts have to do with the supernatural workings of God in the church and in the world.

a. Faith. The God-given ability to rely totally on God for a specific area of concern.

b. Working of miracles. The God-given ability to supersede the natural order to bring glory to God.

c. Healings. The God-given ability to heal people of illness through the power of God.

3. *The revelational gifts.* These three gifts have to do with knowledge into the secrets of God.

a. Discerning of spirits. The God-given ability to determine whether a supernatural manifestation has its source in God or in Satan.

b. Word of wisdom. The God-given ability to know the thoughts of God for the future.

c. Word of knowledge. The God-given ability to know the thoughts of God in the past.

To cover a variety of concerns that people often express about the purpose and operation of the gifts, I will deal with several questions.

"How are the gifts of the Spirit received?"

By faith. The baptism in the Holy Spirit releases within the believer a dynamic which expresses itself in the operation of the gifts. It may help to remember the word *gift* as it appears in 1 Corinthians 12 is a translation of the Greek word *charismata*, "a gift freely and graciously given; a favor bestowed." This is a mighty truth! The gifts of the Spirit operate according to the grace and favor of God. The believer is a channel through whom God's grace flows.

"Are there different uses of unknown tongues?"

Yes. In Acts 2, 10, and 19 tongues appear as an evidence or sign of the infilling of the Holy Spirit. In 1 Corinthians 14:4, 13-15, 18 Paul refers to tongues as a part of the believer's devotional life. And according to 1 Corinthians 14, unknown tongues when interpreted have a use in the assembly to build up and edify the body of Christ.

"Are the gifts of the Spirit for our day?"

Yes. It is impossible to find a point in time when the gifts ceased. We do not find any statement in the Scriptures to suggest the operation of the gifts was limited to apostolic times.

"Aren't the gifts of the Spirit associated with fanaticism?"

The operation of the gifts of the Holy Spirit does involve the emotions very deeply, but that is in no way equal to fanaticism. Any manifestation that could rightly be regarded as fanaticism is without scriptural support. The apostle Paul is very explicit: "Let all things be done properly and in an orderly manner" (1 Corinthians 14:40).

You have the privilege and honor of being used to edify the body of Christ through the operation of the gifts of the Spirit. Don't leave this ministry to others. I like Paul's description of how it all works together: "When you assemble, each one has a psalm, has a teaching, has a revelation, has a tongue, has an interpretation" (1 Corinthians 14:26). Everyone is part of the action!

8   *Your Devotional Life*

Spiritual growth depends on a strong and meaningful relationship with God. Your church life is not enough. You will need to develop your own time for Bible study and prayer.

As life moves on, you will see how much you depend on the inspiration you glean from your own time of meditation and prayer. As helpful and inspiring as worship services are, your spiritual needs and desires will reach beyond the ministry of the church and into your own heart and life of devotion.

The following guidelines will help you in developing your devotional life.

Bible Reading

1. Develop a systematic method for reading the Bible. I like to select a passage from the Historical Books (such as Genesis, 1 Kings), a passage from the Poetical Books (such as Job, Psalms), a passage from the Prophets (such as Isaiah, Joel), a passage from the Gospels, and one from the Epistles. This program of reading and study will allow for flexibility, yet will quickly move you on through the Word.

I personally have a small card on which I record the last chapter I have read in each section. It is a simple yet thorough and balanced approach to Bible reading. Of course, any method of systematic Bible reading that meets your needs is in order.

2. *Learn to meditate on the Word.* The Psalmist said: "I will meditate on Thy precepts, and regard Thy ways. I shall delight in Thy statutes; I shall not forget Thy word" (Psalm 119:15, 16).

Joshua long before was told: "This book of the law shall not depart from your mouth, but you shall meditate on it day and night" (Joshua 1:8).

As you meditate, you will be asking yourself questions like these:

What is revealed here about the character of God?

What did God intend to say to the original readers of this passage?

What does God want to say to me from this part of His Word?

What will I now need to do in response to the Word I have received?

With whom should I share these insights into His Word?

It is through meditation that the glorious truths of God are pointed and planted in our hearts.

3. *Use the Word.* Paul spoke of "the word of faith which we are preaching" (Romans 10:8). An expanded translation of the passage could read: "The word which produces faith which we preach." In other words, the Scriptures themselves produce faith in people's hearts.

There is creative power in the Word. Power to create the likeness of Christ within you. Power to build His church. Power to draw all men to God. And power to live by—so life will be full and meaningful.

Prayer

How can you have a more effective prayer life? Let me offer a few suggestions.

1. Recognize its necessity. It has been said: "Nothing happens except by prayer!" And it is true. The Church does go forward on its knees. Its authority and power are conditioned by the presence or absence of prayer.

2. Set a pattern for prayer. This suggests more than just a regular time and place for prayer. It speaks to the agenda—the components—the functions of effective prayer. The believer who seeks after God in prayer comes in adoration (Psalm 150:1, 2), in confession (Psalm 66:18; 1 John 1:9), in thanksgiving (1 Thessalonians 5:18; Psalm 118:1), and in supplication (James 5:16; Galatians 6:2; Ephesians 6:18).

The sweep of his prayer may include:

Those in leadership around the world;

Those in Spiritual leadership over us;

The city in which God has placed us;

Our nation;

The church to which we are called;

Our immediate family;

The lost with whom we may come in contact;

New converts and needy Christians;

Neighbors on our street;

Those who speak evil against us;

Nations unreached with the gospel;

Brothers and sisters without religious freedom;

The enlarging of our vision and borders of faith;

The nations of the world.

Why not use this list as a guide for intercession? You will quickly see that intercession knows no bounds. It is global in its expression and pointed in its penetration. You will find joy in knowing you have a part in the

51

destiny of nations through the power of prayer. What higher vocation could there be than this?

3. *Support your church in prayer.* You are a key to the successful ministry of your church—and your greatest potential contribution will be in the area of prayer. So many people and circumstances need prayer: the pastor and his staff, the officers and boards, the support staff, the teachers, the ushers, the nursery workers—on and on it goes. This is the field into which you will plant the seed of faith through prayer.

Keep on growing! Growth is imperative. And growth involves change: a change in priorities; a change in life goals; a change in qualities of character; a change in personality; a change in motivation.

Yes, your life in the church will produce change. But it will be positive. You will reflect more and more the radiance of His spotless character. As Paul said: "We all, with unveiled face beholding as in a mirror the glory of the Lord, are being transformed into the same image from glory to glory, just as from the Lord, the Spirit" (2 Corinthians 3:18).

Part 3
Your Church and Its Structure

9 Foundations on Which to Build

With your decision to become a member of the church will also come a curiosity about the history and organization of the church. That is as it ought to be; you need to know.

What are the religious and cultural roots of the Assemblies of God?

How has the church defined its mission during the years of its existence?

What is the organizational structure of the Assemblies of God?

How is the local church structured to fulfill its mission?

National Revivals

Your awareness of the present and future mission of the church will be strongly influenced by your perception of its past. God is a God of history. He has acted decisively in the affairs of men. His plan is beautifully unfolded from Genesis to Revelation. There is progress and movement.

In a sense, the same has been true with our Fellowship. God has graciously moved us along from one level of development to the next. Each has been glorious and fruitful in itself, yet finally yielding to an even greater dimension of service and blessing.

There have been three "great awakenings" in America which have greatly influenced the religious life of this nation and which provide the backdrop for a study of the Pentecostal Movement in our day.

The first great awakening was sparked by the preaching of Jonathan Edwards and George Whitefield. In 1740 revival came to the dead formal churches of New England. People came from miles around and sometimes stood for hours in the rain to hear the anointed ministry of these great men of God.

This visitation was marked with dramatic outward manifestations as the Spirit of conviction took hold of men's hearts.

Unfortunately the revival did not continue. For the next 50 years there was a return to the lifelessness of the earlier period. Yet God had moved. A pattern for revival had been established. It was clear . . . the anointed proclamation of the fundamental truths of the Word brought spiritual life to hungry hearts.

The next great awakening came in 1800, following the Revolutionary War. Large crowds often gathered in tents to spend days in fellowship and spiritual renewal. In some instances local revivals lasted for several years. During this awakening it was not uncommon for people to be so overpowered by the Spirit that they would fall to the floor and remain prostrate for hours. One of the great preachers of this period was Charles G. Finney.

With the financial crash in 1855 people once again began to seek after God, and the great awakening of 1857-58 followed. During this period the Sunday school was born and Fundamentalism popularized. Small prayer groups sprang up as people longed to know God.

There were literally thousands of converts during this revival.

Since the awakening of 1857-58 America has not again experienced a national revival. With the advent of the Civil War people turned their minds to other things, and the revival fires began to diminish. To this day America still waits for a revival that will touch its borders and affect its national life.

But that is not the whole story. Although more limited in scope, the Pentecostal outpouring at the turn of the century has brought new life to the church and hope again for a revival that will sweep America. It is to a consideration of that Movement that we now turn.

The Holiness Movement

In 1859 Charles Darwin published a book outlining his theory of evolution. Arguing for a scientific explanation for the origin of man, he succeeded in bringing into question the Biblical account of Creation.

In the same spirit Sigmund Freud advanced new theories of psychology that attempted to show sin not as an offense against God's moral law but as merely the outcropping of a natural response to the forces of environment. These two men did much to lay the foundation for humanism.

The church responded to this onslaught of pseudointellectualism by accommodating itself to it. The church turned away from the simple gospel of the apostles to a gospel based on social demands. It sought an explanation of Biblical truth from a scientific point of view.

The end result was subjecting the Bible to the whims and wishes of men's critical thinking. The authenticity of the Biblical documents was brought into question; the miracles of Jesus were explained from a nonsupernatural perspective; and the Bible in general was treated as a collection of myths. The church understandably lost its fervor, and its vision of mission became pathetically blurred.

This new liberalism was, fortunately, not without its challenge. Running parallel with it was a movement that has become known as the holiness movement. In reaction to the cold and heartless liberalism that had swept the church, the holiness people sought to recapture the gospel proclaimed by the apostles. They believed the Bible was indeed the Word of God. They believed in the miracles of Jesus. They believed the mission of the church was to purge itself of worldliness and to preach the gospel around the world.

The holiness movement was the seedbed from which the Pentecostal Movement could spring.

The Pentecostal Revival

In 1900 at Topeka, Kansas, a group of Bible school students began to search the Scriptures for an understanding of the baptism in the Holy Spirit. After several days of waiting, they were filled with the Spirit and began to speak with other tongues. It was clearly a return to the apostolic experience.

Within a few days visiting pastors had arrived at the Bible school, and they too shared the joys of the "Pentecostal experience." From that humble beginning the spiritual fires of renewal leaped across the nation and around the world. Thousands of believers received the baptism in the Holy Spirit with the evidence of speaking in other tongues. The Pentecostal Movement, so well known in our day, had begun.

The Birth of a Church

By 1914 the need for structure became apparent. Since the historical churches looked with criticism on the new movement, the early Pentecostal people had little choice but to band together and seek God for His direction in forming a cooperative fellowship.

In April 1914, 300 Pentecostal leaders met in Hot Springs, Arkansas to set in order the General Council of the Assemblies of God. There were five major concerns: (1) doctrinal unity, (2) a method by which the results of evangelism could be preserved, (3) the development of a program for world missions, (4) the proper legal structure of the church, and (5) the establishment of a Bible school program for the training of workers.

It was not until the fourth General Council, held in St. Louis, Missouri in 1916, that a formal Statement of Fundamental Truths was adopted. The statement was not intended to be a comprehensive statement of all Biblical truths, but rather the setting forth of those truths deemed necessary for a distinctive and effective ministry in the world.

That early statement has served us well throughout the years and has been the catalyst to bring Pentecostal people together from a variety of theological backgrounds. By 1917 the Fellowship included 517 ministers and 56 foreign missionaries. From then until now the Assemblies of God has enjoyed a steady growth to become the largest Pentecostal group in the world and a major force among evangelicals.

Two independent Pentecostal papers served as the early voice of the Fellowship: the *Word and Witness*, a monthly paper edited by E. N. Bell, the *The Christian Evangel*, a weekly edited by J. Roswell Flower. The two papers merged into what was eventually called the *Pen-

tecostal Evangel. This publication has been the voice of the Assemblies of God since that time and is one of the most widely circulated Protestant weeklies in the U.S.

The headquarters for the Assemblies of God was first located in Findlay, Ohio. After several months it was moved to St. Louis, Missouri, following the decision of the second General Council. In 1919 larger quarters were needed, and a building in Springfield, Missouri was acquired. It provided space for the executive offices, editorial and service personnel, and a distribution center. When the volume of work made it necessary to expand, a new location was chosen in Springfield. First a building to house the printing operations was built, then an office complex, and next a distribution center. The headquarters, located at 1445 Boonville in Springfield, serves the worldwide ministries of the Assemblies of God and employs some 800 persons. The printing operation is one of the largest religious printing operations in the world.

Structure of the Assemblies of God

The Assemblies of God was organized to provide the guidelines for a cooperative fellowship of Pentecostal people who shared a common spiritual experience and a common vision to evangelize the world. Each church was to enjoy its own sovereignty and be self-governing. The congregational form of government was adopted, placing the responsibility for decisionmaking in the hands of individual members of the local assembly.

The leaders of the Fellowship are prepared to assist the local church in selecting a pastor, helping to set in order new assemblies, counseling assemblies that may be in disunity, and offering to each pastor an opportunity for fellowship with other pastors and church leaders.

The service departments of the church provide literature, organizational helps, inspirational conferences and seminars, and a variety of other services for the local church.

The General Council of the Assemblies of God in the United States is divided into 57 districts. Each district has its own superintendent, secretary-treasurer, and district presbytery (comprised of sectional or area presbyters). The district superintendents along with two other elected officials from each district form the General Presbytery of the General Council.

The Executive Presbytery, to whom is entrusted the overall operation of the Fellowship, is comprised of the general superintendent, assistant general superintendent, general secretary, general treasurer, executive director of foreign missions, and eight other elected representatives.

There is within the Fellowship flexibility, diversity, individual creativity, and personal initiative. These qualities of spirit and attitude comprise a great resource. The Fellowship provides the necessary parameters and guidelines to undergird and encourage the work of the local church.

The Assemblies of God has continued to grow until in recent years its worldwide adherents total over 10 million.

10   The Structure of the Local Church

Because of the diversity within the Assemblies of God and the sovereignty of each local church, it follows that each church will have its own constitution and bylaws.

Your pastor will likely provide you with a copy of the constitution and bylaws for your assembly. Your familiarity with this document will help you act wisely as you share in the decisionmaking process of the church.

Constitution and Bylaws

Following is a brief summary of some of the fundamental provisions usually found in the constitution and bylaws of the local church.

1. The doctrinal statement. The doctrinal statement of the Assemblies of God will be included. Both pastors and local churches are expected to find agreement on the statement and affirm the same.

2. The choice of leaders. The constitution and bylaws will set forth the manner in which the church will choose its leaders. The procedure to be followed in selecting a pastor, his term of office, his responsibilities, and the provisions for termination will be included. The requirements for the other officers (deacons/trustees), their term of office, their responsibilities, and the provisions for the termination of their term will be set forth.

Included also will be directives to be followed in the selection of officers for the various departments of the church. The constitution and bylaws of the local church will spell out the necessary guidelines for maintaining adequate leadership in the church.

3. *Ownership of property.* The document will specify the manner in which the local church may own and dispose of property, both real and chattel.

4. *Membership.* Each church will establish its own conditions for membership. Those conditions will usually include: (a) the clear testimony of the new life in Jesus Christ; (b) a commitment to live the Christian life before the world; (c) an expressed willingness to adhere to the fundamental teachings of the church; and (d) an affirmation of Biblical principles of stewardship. The constitution and bylaws will also spell out the rights and privileges of membership as well as the conditions by which a member may be discharged.

5. *The conducting of business.* Who is allowed to vote? When will the church conduct its business? What will be its agenda? Who will serve as the chairman? What part of the membership must be present to constitute a quorum? How is the meeting to be announced to the membership? These and other related questions will find answers in the constitution and bylaws of the local church.

6. *The guidelines for the departments.* Many local churches will include the necessary provisions for the creation and operation of departments within the church. Youth, Women's Ministries, Men's Ministries, Music, Sunday school, Royal Rangers, and Missionettes are typical of the departments found in most Assemblies of God churches.

Doctrinal Considerations

Before moving on to other matters that pertain to structure, it will be helpful to consider several principles to help you understand why it is important to preserve sound doctrine in the local church.

1. Doctrine must be based on the Scriptures as understood in their historical, cultural, and grammatical context.

2. Know what you believe but have a spirit of charity toward those who differ with you. The church is needlessly divided by those who insist on doctrinal purity established by their own criteria. Seek a common ground of agreement in Jesus Christ and His lordship, both within the local church and in relationship to the body of Christ at large.

A nasty spirit of argumentation and controversy is not needed in the church. Know what you believe and why you believe it—and then have a big heart toward those who disagree with you on those points of doctrine nonessential to true fellowship in Jesus Christ.

3. Accept the fact of paradox in the Scriptures. We believe the Bible is the inspired, infallible, and inerrant Word of God to men in all matters of faith, practice, religious experience, and text itself.

All Scripture is inspired by God and profitable for teaching, for reproof, for correction, for training in righteousness; that the man of God may be adequate, equipped for every good work" (2 Timothy 3:16, 17).

Sometimes we may be confronted with what appears to be an inconsistency or contradiction. In such cases we should be content to leave the matter for further meditation and study. The Scriptures cannot be subjected to a criterion of logic alone. Humility of heart, spirit, and mind are requisites to good interpretation.

4. Understand the central place of grace. Man is justified before God by faith and through grace; not by his own efforts or his inherent goodness. Remember this formula: Faith plus zero equals salvation.

Ask the religious solicitor at the door: "How is a man justified—declared righteous before God?" And if he answers with any other statement than, "By faith in the finished work of Christ," you will know that teaching is in error.

Our nature seeks ways in which we may establish our own righteousness. We want desperately to impress God—to work out our own salvation. But God says we are justified through faith in the finished work of Christ. It is far more important to speak of what God has done than what man can ever do. Keep this in focus, and you will discern between truth and error.

5. Appreciate the significance of great doctrinal truths held by the Church for centuries. As part of a contemporary revival movement, we must not lose sight of those basic Biblical and doctrinal truths which, though hidden in obscurity at times, have still been held and affirmed by the Church: justification by faith, the inspiration of the Scriptures, the Triune God, the Virgin Birth, and the physical resurrection of Jesus, just to mention a few. An emphasis here will avoid a shallow kind of religious faith.

6. Avoid doctrinal controversy and argument. The church of Jesus Christ has been splintered time and time again by the cutting edge of doctrinal controversy. Could it be that doctrinal statements have sometimes been used more to tear apart than unite? Have men sometimes hidden their rebellion and hatred behind

doctrines and dogmas? It is time now to allow the Holy Spirit to bring the body of Christ together in a strong affirmation of fundamental Biblical truths—and He is in our day.

Four Cardinal Truths

Here are four basic truths set forth by the Assemblies of God:

1. Salvation through the shed blood of Jesus Christ. We believe man is lost and without hope outside of Jesus Christ. How can his state be altered? How can fellowship be regained? The Bible says only by faith in the shed blood of Christ.

We believe therefore in the new birth—that instantaneously, through faith, a person can become a new creature in Christ. And we believe also in the continuous work of the Holy Spirit to sanctify, purify, and restore to fellowship with God those who believe.

2. The baptism in the Holy Spirit. Though previously dealt with at some length, it is good in this context to point out we believe in a definite work of the Holy Spirit subsequent to conversion. The pattern is clear in Acts 2, 10, and 19. In each case believers were filled with the Holy Spirit and spoke with tongues as the Holy Spirit gave them the ability.

3. Divine healing. Isaiah the prophet said: "He was crushed for our iniquities. . . . And by His scourging we are healed" (Isaiah 53:5). Jesus died to atone for sin and to provide healing from disease and sickness. James instructed the church in implementing this truth: "Call for the elders of the church . . . pray over him, anointing him with oil in the name of the Lord" (James 5:14). This truth continues to be experienced in the Church in our day.

4. The imminent and physical return of Jesus Christ.
As a Fellowship we believe in the soon coming of the
Lord Jesus Christ. We take Paul's words to be literally
and gloriously true:

> For the Lord Himself will descend from heaven with a
> shout, with the voice of the archangel, and with the trumpet of
> God; and the dead in Christ shall rise first. Then we who are
> alive and remain shall be caught up together with them in the
> clouds to meet the Lord in the air (1 Thessalonians 4:16, 17).

We believe further that following the gathering of the
Church unto Christ there will be on earth a 1000-year
period of peace. Isaiah had a vision of this time:

> And the wolf will dwell with the lamb, and the leopard will
> lie down with the kid, and the calf and the young lion and the
> fatling together; and a little boy will lead them. . . . They will
> not hurt or destroy in all My holy mountain, for the earth will
> be full of the knowledge of the Lord as the waters cover the sea
> (Isaiah 11:6, 9).

(See appendix for our complete Statement of Fundamental Truths.)

Leadership

The constitution and bylaws deal with the matter of
leadership and governance for the local church. The
subject of leadership will be viewed here as it has to do
with the pastor (or pastors), the board of deacons and
trustees, and such departmental leaders as may be
elected by the membership.

1. The pastor. He or she is the God-appointed leader
of the local church. Though usually elected by the
membership of the congregation, the pastor is first the
servant of Christ called to minister to the body of

Christ. The pastor's authority is God-given, but it is exercised in humility and servitude. The pastor's supreme example is the Lord himself who came not to be ministered unto, but to minister.

It is the pastor's responsibility to give direction to the activities and affairs of the church. He will seek counsel and assistance from the official board and other leaders within the church, but finally he bears the responsibility for the well-being of the church.

He will be expected to serve the people of God both by word and by example; his spirit should be that of Christ's.

You will find him to be subject to the same temptations that come to everyone; he will bear the same marks of imperfection that are seen in the lives of others. Still he is God's servant, appointed to inspire and lead the church of Jesus Christ.

I list here what you may expect of him (and other pastors who may be working with him):

a. That he will seek the Lord for wisdom in leading the church.

b. That he will regularly present the Word of God in an anointed, interesting, challenging, and practical manner.

c. That he will assist you in counseling, prayer, and visitation.

d. That he will hold confidences that you may entrust to him.

e. That he will help you to grow in your walk with Christ and your service for the Kingdom.

f. That he will seek to serve as a model for the Christian life—yet living before you in honesty and openness, willing to share both victories and defeats.

I list now what he may expect of you:

a. That you will be faithful in attending the services of the church and in receiving Communion.

b. That you will seek to live out the messages he gives from the Word both in attitude and in conduct.

c. That you will support the worldwide ministry of the church through the practice of Biblical principles of stewardship.

d. That you will speak well of his ministry and of the church.

e. That you will share your positive concerns with him for the growth and health of the body.

f. That you will regularly pray for his personal spiritual growth, his public ministry, and the well-being of his family.

The relationship you enjoy with your pastor is potentially one of the most positive and helpful relationships you will encounter. You are drawn together by a common vision, you share a common spiritual experience, and you are cooperating in a common task—to reach the world for Christ. Neither you nor he should settle for less than a healthy, positive, Christ-honoring relationship.

2. The board of deacons and trustees. These are two specific offices spoken of in the New Testament. One is deacon *(diakonos,* "one who serves") and the other is elder *(presbuteros,* "older man, elder") or bishop *(episkopos,* "overseer or bishop").

The office of deacon is patterned in Acts 6 when the need for the care of the widows became apparent to the Twelve:

It is not desirable for us to neglect the word of God in order to serve tables. But select from among you, brethren, seven men of good reputation, full of the Spirit and of wisdom, whom we may put in charge of this task (Acts 6:2, 3).

The need for deacons is also a modern demand placed on the church by the corporate laws of various states. But the point is clear: The apostles understood their first duty to be prayer and the ministry of the Word, and that others be appointed to carry on the duties of a caring and ministering fellowship. (The requirements for a deacon are outlined in 1 Timothy 3:8-10.)

The office of elder is patterned in Acts 14 where it describes the church-planting program of the apostle Paul: "And when they had appointed elders for them in every church, having prayed with fasting, they commended them to the Lord in whom they had believed" (v. 23).

The terms *elder* and *bishop* appear to be used interchangeably in the New Testament. The term *bishop* speaks more of office and the term *elder* of function and ministry. In most Assemblies of God churches the pastor or pastors serve as the elder or elders. But more recently some churches have recognized those persons who meet the qualifications set forth in 1 Timothy 3:1-7 and Titus 2:2 as elders in the church. Usually they serve with the pastor in spiritual ministry to the church and do not comprise an administrative board as such. Some churches combine the responsibilities of deacons and elders.

In any event, the board of deacons/trustees will work with the pastor in all matters having to do with the operation and ministry of the church. Listed here are some of their duties:

a. To serve the people of the church in their spiritual growth and development.

b. To counsel with the pastor in matters pertaining to the assembly.

c. To set policy on budgetary matters.

d. To work with the pastor in providing the necessary staff to assure the efficient operation of the church.

e. To provide for the construction and upkeep of the church facility.

f. To share in the articulation of the vision and mission of the church.

g. To serve as models of Christlikeness before the church and before the world.

The local church will be only as strong as its leaders. When the church is blessed with leadership that has vision, commitment, and practical know-how, that church will prosper on every front.

You will want to pray continuously for the development of strong and dynamic leadership within the church.

Departments

These are the major departments within a typical Assemblies of God church.

1. *Sunday school department.* Christian education is a high priority in our churches. Most provide a Bible class appropriate for every person regardless of age. The classes usually meet simultaneously at a convenient hour on Sunday mornings. Here the Word of God is taught, the Christian life modeled, and the opportunity for dynamic Christian fellowship provided.

The Sunday school, by virtue of its function, becomes a major part of the evangelistic outreach of the local church.

2. *Youth department.* Each church should develop a ministry to youth compatible with its needs and consistent with its vision. Typically, the youth program of the local church includes a weekly total-group service, regular social-type gatherings, and various kinds of

evangelism-outreach programs. The impact of a dynamic youth program is felt throughout the entire church. The youth are not the church of tomorrow—they are the church today. Frequently they use the name *Christ's Ambassadors*.

3. Women's Ministries. The women of the church are mobilized to support the missionary program of the church through giving, serving, and prayer, and to undergird the total work of the local church. You will find these women providing necessary household and personal items for missionaries, preparing the meal for a special all-church fellowship banquet, sending clothing to needy families within the community, visiting the members of the Fellowship who are ill, and writing letters of encouragement to the missionary team of the church.

4. Men's Ministries. A church in South America is built by a group of men from an Assemblies of God church in the U.S. A community crusade is planned in a U.S. city to reach people for Christ and is implemented by the men of a local assembly. An evening of fellowship is planned for all the men and boys of the church. And the variety of activities of the Men's Ministries reaches far beyond what is suggested here.

5. Missionettes and Royal Rangers. These two groups could have been listed under the Men's and Women's Ministries, since each is organizationally to be found there. Yet they do deserve separate treatment. Besides the graded Sunday school program, most churches provide a weekly activity-oriented program for boys and girls. Hiking, camping, cooking, sewing, crafts, Bible study, and Scripture memorization are some of the activities of the respective groups. The programs are designed to build faith and character through guided activities and modeled Christian living.

6. *Music.* Music has a place in every department of the church. Song leaders, accompanists, graded choirs, orchestras, vocal and instrumental solos and ensembles, all contribute to the music ministry of the church, coordinated by the music department.

Now that you have looked at the basic organizational structure of your church, you will undoubtedly feel better prepared to find your place in a wonderful fellowship of God's people.

Part 4
Your Church and Its Mission

11   Upward in Worship

If you're looking for action, you will find it in the church.

What is more exhilarating than spontaneous worship? What can compare with the good feeling that comes when you know someone really cares? And where can you find a higher level of motivation than that which comes with the call to win the whole world for Christ?

Museums have many nice articles, but they are just to be viewed. Do not touch!

Athletic contests make the heart beat faster and excite the nervous system, but the action is on the field.

Television makes the world so small it will fit in your front room, but it's a one-way street. The box can't listen.

And so it is with the world around us. There is little heart. The individual doesn't count for much. The many are lost in favor of an honored few. "Look—don't touch" is more than a protective slogan for merchandise. People are spectators. The real action is somehow beyond reach.

The church is the counter to all of this. Here you count—because you are it, the church. People care; they listen and share. It is a family place. No one is worth less or more than anyone else.

The Assemblies of God considers that it has a three-fold mission: ministry to the Lord, to the saints, and to the unconverted. This chapter will look at the church's worship—its ministry to the Lord.

The church is at its best when it has come together to worship. It is the church's finest hour. From every part of town, from every walk of life, and from every interest group they come, drawn by an urge to worship God in spirit and truth and to share their joy with others.

What is *worship?* The word itself means "worthship," the ascription of value to one honored and revered. It is a translation of the Hebrew word which means "bow down, prostrate," and a Greek word which means "to prostrate, do obeisance to."

Though used occasionally of men, the term is most often and appropriately used of God. It has to do with the acknowledgment of God's perfectness and unspeakable glory.

In the Scriptures worship is found in four developmental stages. Prior to the tabernacle of Moses, no lines were drawn between public and private worship. During this period worship was unstructured and highly personal.

With the advent of the tabernacle first and then the temple, worship became more highly complex, centering in the rites and rituals carried on by the priests and Levites.

Decentralization took place during the Exile, and the synagogue became the place of worship. Wherever Jewish people were found, synagogues sprang up. The emphasis in the synagogue was more on instruction than worship. This is understandable in light of the pressures placed on traditions by hostile nations.

The last stage of development is seen in the early Christian church.

Public worship in the Early Church consisted of the following.

1. Preaching (Acts 20:7). 2. Reading the Scriptures (James 1:22). 3. Prayer (1 Corinthians 14:15). 4. Singing (Ephesians 5:19). 5. Water baptism (Acts 2:41). 6. Communion (Acts 2:42. See also the full exposition on the Lord's Supper in 1 Corinthians 11:18-34.). 7. Stewardship (1 Corinthians 16:2). 8. Operation of the gifts (1 Corinthians 14:26).

Let us look at each of these.

Preaching

Yes, preaching is one of the ways in which God is worshiped. The spoken word, finding affirmation in the heart of the worshiper, returns to its Source as worship. This calls for active and creative listening. The pulpit and the pew come together—and God is exalted in worship.

The health of the church depends on good preaching. Paul understood this when he explained: "But we preach Christ crucified, to Jews a stumbling block, and to Gentiles foolishness, but to those who are the called . . . Christ the power of God and the wisdom of God" (1 Corinthians 1:23, 24). Preaching is God's way of saving the lost and building the church.

Your spiritual growth will be strongly influenced by the preaching ministry of your church. You will want to develop the ability to be a good listener. Devise a way to retain the major points of a message and structure a set of criteria for evaluating each message as to whether it is scriptural and practical. Your pastor wants nothing less. He works diligently and prayerfully to give you the message God has for you, but he does not want you to be passive and uncritical as you listen.

You will be enriched by the faithful preaching of your pastor. Listen intently. Write down the major points. Find ways to put the truths to work in your life. Share the message with others. And, most of all, let each message make you more like Jesus Christ in the way you think, speak, and act.

Reading the Scriptures

The example of the Jesus is most instructive: "And He came to Nazareth, where He had been brought up; and as was His custom, He entered the synagogue on the Sabbath, and stood up to read" (Luke 4:16). This was the pattern for synagogue worship. The Scriptures were read and then expounded: "And He began to say to them, 'Today this Scripture has been fulfilled in your hearing' " (v. 21).

Times of great spiritual awakening have always involved reading the Word. Reading the Word sparked revival in Josiah's day. Martin Luther's discovery of truth was the result of reading the Scriptures. The great revivals of our day have inevitably been a rediscovery of God's power through the Word. Is it any wonder then that God blesses any group of believers who will honor His Word?

In what way may the public reading of the Word be considered worship? After comparing the Word with the life-giving properties of falling rain and snow, the Lord says:

So shall My word be which goes forth from My mouth; it shall not return to Me empty, without accomplishing what I desire, and without succeeding in the matter for which I sent it (Isaiah 55:11).

Who returns the Word? Could it be God intends that His Word be "sent forth" through its reading and that its return be through the response of worship in the hearts of His people?

Prayer

The Psalmist has given us an example of the variety, substance, and spirit of prayer.

The prayer of trust: "In peace I will both lie down and sleep, for Thou alone, O Lord, dost make me to dwell in safety" (Psalm 4:8).

The prayer for protection: "O Lord, lead me in Thy righteousness because of my foes; make Thy way straight before me" (Psalm 5:8).

The prayer for mercy: "Return, O Lord, rescue my soul; save me because of Thy lovingkindness" (Psalm 6:4).

The prayer for defense from enemies: "Save me from all those who pursue me, and deliver me" (Psalm 7:1).

The prayer of thanksgiving: "I will give thanks to the Lord with all my heart; I will tell of all Thy wonders" (Psalm 9:1).

The prayer for guidance: "Make me know Thy ways, O Lord; teach me Thy paths" (Psalm 25:4).

The prayer for forgiveness: "Wash me thoroughly from my iniquity, and cleanse me from my sin" (Psalm 51:2).

The prayer of praise: "O sing to the Lord a new song, for He has done wonderful things, His right hand and His holy arm have gained the victory for Him" (Psalm 98:1).

Strikingly absent here is vain repetition and hypocrisy. The Psalmist simply talked to God. He used ordinary speech and common thought patterns. His prayers rose out of his experience with God and his participation in the ordinary events of life. The reader is repeatedly struck with the content and substance of the Psalmist's prayers—they are expressions of a man in touch with God, with himself, and with his world.

Prayer is worship. It is the believer's expression of his deepest emotions of love, gratitude, and reverence. In prayer the believer touches the limitlessness of God's power and the unsurpassable majesty of His glory. He is drawn into a relationship of intimacy and communion. The divine and human find a point of contact—worship is the consequence of that encounter.

Seek to develop your prayer life. Analyze the great prayers of the Bible for example and pattern. Be creative. Avoid cliches and repetitious forms. Stay close to your own experiences in life for the content of prayer. Let prayer be ever new and refreshing. Let it be the expression of your deepest feelings to God. Use the language of life—the expressions of the everyday—the thoughts that are familiar, to express your worship through prayer.

The church gathered to pray. What could be more glorious than that?

Don't be a spectator, standing by as an observer to others who are approaching God in prayer. Find a place of agreement. Let the prayer that is being offered become your own expression to the Lord. Corporate prayer will then rise to God like a symphony of song and praise.

Public prayer is troublesome for some people. They feel distracted when they hear others in audible prayer and praise. Perhaps the following guidelines will be helpful:

1. *Do not seek to be heard of men.* The audible level will sometimes be high and at other times low. There will be times of great exuberance—a mighty shout unto the Lord—and times when God will visit the utter silence of His people. At either level your voice should blend and be in harmony with the voices of the other worshipers.

2. *Do not equate intensity of emotion in prayer with the real power of prayer.* Some people think the effectiveness of prayer rises according to its level of intensity. God looks on the heart. The power of prayer is measured more in terms of *faith* than force. A highly intense and emotional prayer may be uttered in a heartless way. And a prayer of great faith and power may be offered in a whisper.

3. *Do not forget about your neighbor.* The man standing at your side may be in church for the first time in years—and perhaps the only type of religious service he has ever known has been highly ritualistic and formal. You will need to keep him in mind as you express yourself in worship. If the pattern for worship through prayer and praise is in balance with the Word of God, even the stranger will know it is of God. Granted, he may have feelings of hostility, but in his heart something good and positive will have occurred. Remember, true freedom and liberty of the Holy Spirit are never confusing and disorderly.

All this is brought into focus in these words: "Again I say to you, that if two of you agree on earth about anything that they may ask, it shall be done for them by My Father who is in heaven" (Matthew 18:19). The word *agree* is the translation of the Greek word *symphoneo*, meaning "to sound together, to harmonize." And that is what public praise and prayer is all about— a harmonious expression to God of His greatness, glory, and incarnate love.

Singing

Music is a vital part of the worship life of the church. Some have said you may measure the spiritual vitality of a church by analyzing its music. And that is likely true. Why? Because music expresses human experience. It is somehow a measure of what is in the spirit. A church expresses itself in victorious song when its experience in God is jubilant and triumphant.

What are some of the distinguishing marks of a music ministry you can usually expect in the local church?

1. Variety. Music appreciation is conditioned by age, ethnic and cultural background, and geographical origin. The local church will seek to accommodate itself to the wide variety in music appreciation among its members as much as is possible and right.

2. Ministry-centered. Music that is properly chosen and presented will minister to the needs of the people and will bring glory to the Lord. Musicians have been given a powerful tool to enrich the work of God. Many have come to Christ through anointed gospel music.

3. Participatory. Music is not the property of a few select and talented musicians. God has put a song in the heart of every person. The Psalmist caught the spirit of this truth:

Praise Him with trumpet sound; praise Him with harp and lyre. Praise Him with timbrel and dancing; praise Him with stringed instruments and pipe. Praise Him with loud cymbals; praise Him with resounding cymbals. Let everything that has breath praise the Lord" (Psalm 150:3-6).

4. Biblical. The Book of Psalms was the songbook of Israel. In our day many of the great passages of the Bible have been put to music. People have spoken repeatedly of the great blessing that has come to them through singing God's Word.

5. *New.* This is an attribute of God—He is ever new. He does new things (Isaiah 43:19); His mercies are new every morning (Lamentations 3:23); His plan for the ages involves a new heaven and a new earth (Revelation 21:1); and He has put within man a new song: "I will sing a new song to Thee, O God; Upon a harp of ten strings I will sing praises to Thee" (Psalm 144:9).

Here is a dynamic and creative way for you to express your worship unto the Lord. Use your musical abilities, undeveloped as they may be, to declare your love and adoration to the Lord. Remember, God is not so much concerned about the quality of your musical expression; He just wants you to glorify Him.

Water Baptism

Water baptism is a public pledge of a heart commitment to Christ. The Early Church understood it as the "initiation" into Christian faith. It was the occasion whereby the new believer declared to the world that Jesus Christ would now be Lord. Persecution often hinged on whether or not a believer had been baptized. Death was sometimes the consequence of water baptism.

You will find a baptismal service provides the occasion for a meaningful and inspiring worship experience. The testimonies of faith, the identification with Christ in His death and resurrection symbolized through immersion, and the expressions of praise and worship that accompany the baptismal service will prompt deep emotions of worship within your heart.

Communion

The apostle Paul established the basic meaning of the Communion service in 1 Corinthians 10:16. The Greek word translated "fellowship" in *The Amplified Bible* literally means "the act of sharing." In the Communion service believers symbolically share the body and blood of Jesus Christ. It is a service marked with participation.

1. Jesus is present in the Communion service. But in what sense? Are the bread and wine physically and essentially transformed into the body and blood of Christ (called transubstantiation)? Or is the transformation mystical (called consubstantiation) instead of physical and essential? We do not believe either is right. Jesus intended but one thing—that believers (the body of Christ) would recognize His special presence in the Communion service—the bread and wine, being understood symbolically, represent that presence.

2. The Communion service is the Spirit's way to preserve unity in the Body. The believer is admonished to examine himself prior to participation to assure his preparedness. If he is made aware of sin in his life, he must then confess that sin and, when necessary, make restitution with an offended brother.

The Communion service is meant to preserve unity in the body of Christ. It is untenable to imagine persistent participation in it when animosity and hatred have divided the Body. Sooner or later conviction will do its compelling work, and repentant believers will find unity again in Christ.

3. The Communion service provides the occasion for ministry to the members of the Body. Prayer for the sick, the operation of the gifts of the Spirit, and the ministry of encouragement between members should be a part of the Communion service. The body of Christ, in its composite, will be strengthened as these ministries occur.

4. The Communion service is a celebration. The Holy Spirit waits to move freely and dynamically in your heart. It will happen if your attitude is one of openness, honesty, and sincerity.

5. The Communion service is a memorial. As we participate in the Communion service we remember our Lord's suffering and death (1 Corinthians 11:25, 26).

Your walk with the Lord and your positive relationship with the other members of the church will be enhanced and enlarged as you participate fully in Communion. As you do, you are joining the Church of every age in declaring its faith and hope in the living Christ.

Stewardship

Worship is the only right motive for giving. Offerings are given as an act of worship unto the Lord. With joy, faith, and hope the believer presents his offering unto the Lord.

As he gives, he separates himself from his gift and from its use. He does not present his gift as a symbol of status or as an instrument of control. His gift is unto the Lord. Concerns for its use are expressed only in the context of total-membership actions or as relates to the stewardship responsibilities of the church itself.

Confusion on this point has prompted believers to give or refuse to give according to their personal assessment of the potential use or misuse of their gifts rather than in obedience to Christ and as an act of worship. The two are separate considerations.

Operation of the Gifts

In chapter 7 the gifts of the Spirit were identified and their purpose described. It is adequate here simply to stress that the spiritual gifts are indeed a vital part of the worship life of the church. The gifts provide the means whereby the members of the body of Christ minister to one another in the power of the Holy Spirit for edification, correction, and encouragement.

Your pastor will seek to create an atmosphere in which the gifts may freely operate. You will want to be sensitive to the leadership of the Holy Spirit through him as he guides the church in the operation of the gifts. It is his responsibility to spare the church from abusive and unscriptural expressions that seek entrance under the guise of spirituality. "Freedom with control" is not an idiom of contradiction—it is exactly what a church, in pattern after the Early Church, will demand of itself.

There are other references to worship that have to do with attitude and spirit. They also need to be included in our study.

1. Holiness (Psalm 96:9). 2. Giving (1 Chronicles 16:29). 3. Humility (Psalm 95:6). 4. Singleheartedness (Matthew 4:10). 5. Sincerity (John 4:24). 6. God-centeredness (Revelation 14:7). 7. Togetherness (Isaiah 2:3). 8. Love (Psalm 26:8). 9. Joy (Psalm 122:1). 10. Praise (Psalm 84:4). 11. Repentance (Isaiah 37:1).

God alone is worthy of our worship.

12   *Inward in Commitment*

Without member commitment, the church ceases to exist. I do not mean so much commitment to the ministry of the church as I do the personal commitment members must make to each other.

Can you really say the church exists if its life involves nothing more than a once-a-week time of inspiration sandwiched into a busy and hectic week? I doubt you can. The church, by definition and pattern, is a group of believers who have covenanted together to live the Christ life in relationship to each other and to the world.

It is time the church begins to live out its proclamation. When it speaks of love, it must be a showpiece of love. When it speaks of forgiveness, it must show the world the mechanics of reconciliation. When it speaks of spiritual power, it must demonstrate that power through transformed living.

This is what the church is all about. It is time the veil be rent again—this time in the temple of men's hearts.

The Early Church enjoyed a quality of life worthy of duplication. Luke the historian describes it:

And all those who had believed were together, and had all things in common; and they began selling their property and possessions, and were sharing them with all, as anyone might have need. And day by day continuing with one mind in the temple, and breaking bread from house to house, they were taking their meals together with gladness and sincerity of heart, praising God, and having favor with all the people. And the Lord was adding to their number day by day those who were being saved (Acts 2:44-47).

What principles might be extracted from this passage that would speak to the church today?

Jesus Was Its Focus

The early Christians believed the gospel and in that belief found a common ground for their togetherness.

The same is true today. The church is comprised of persons representing a variety of vocational, economic, educational, and cultural interests. Only Jesus Christ is adequate to diminish all differences and bring oneness to a body of believers. The rich and poor, wise and foolish, learned and unlearned, young and old, all find in Christ a spirit of commonness and unity. In the church the ground is level—for group identification is in Christ alone.

Sharing Was Its Essence

A spirit of sharing is essential to the vibrant life of the church. The first-century believers surrendered title to all possessions and held them to be common. While necessity may not now demand such action, the principle is nonetheless applicable. The believer understands his life is not his own, but is Christ's, and so is everything in life to which he holds title. At any moment he must be willing to relinquish what he has for a higher cause.

This has a broader point of reference than mere material commodities. The believer is called to hold loosely all that is his—whether talents and aspirations or material possessions—and be willing to yield them up for the benefit of the body of Christ.

What is said here is not intended to suggest the church today should seek to pattern itself after the Jerusalem church of the first century in matters of economics. It only means the same spirit of self-giving must prevail in the church today as it did then. Cultural demands will vary from one generation to the next. Our day may call for different kinds of accommodations—no less costly perhaps and just as essential to the church's survival.

In both cases the call is for self-giving and a spirit of sharing. Consider the pressures of a demanding schedule or the scarcity of time in a rushing world. Modern life militates against the spirit of self-disclosure and mutuality that so dramatically characterized the life of the Early Church.

You must face the reality of this principle in your own life. You have been called to a life of participation and fellowship. Giving is the axis on which it turns. And in giving you will receive—far above measure or imagination. It is the life worth living.

Worship Was Its Expression

The Early Church continued to worship in the temple as had been the custom. But now worship began to occur in house meetings as well. The people gathered for prayer, praise, study, and fellowship around the table of the Lord.

Worship and fellowship are no less essential in our day. The writer to the Hebrews put the matter in clear focus: "Not forsaking our own assembling together, as is the habit of some, but encouraging one another; and all the more, as you see the day drawing near" (Hebrews 10:25).

Your spiritual growth will depend on your faithful attendance in the place of worship. And your ministry to the other members of the fellowship necessitates your presence when the church comes together. To put it pointedly, faithfulness in attendance is a mandate of the Word and a demand of the fellowship to which you have been called.

Gladness Was Its Spirit

Gladness and joy are the by-products of living together in the church. There is no trace of drudgery in the historical record. The early worshipers gathered with rejoicing and glad hearts. They went from house to house praising, singing, and celebrating the victory of Christ. Nothing less will do in our day.

Growth Was Its Inevitability

How does a church grow? What is the secret? The answer is clear—a healthy organism will continually and naturally be reproducing itself. There is at work within it a life principle. Growth is inevitable.

So it was in the Early Church. "The Lord was adding to their number day by day those who were being saved" (Acts 2:47). The inner life of the church had an arresting appeal that assured the Early Church of continual growth. This is still the key to church growth.

You are being asked to make a commitment to that part of the body of Christ to which you have been called. You are being asked to live in truth and righteousness, to share your life with others, to be open to correction and to correct, to support the body with loyalty and love, to share its vision, and to help realize its aspirations. You are the church!

John said: "If we walk in the light as He Himself is in the light, we have fellowship with one another, and the blood of Jesus His Son cleanses us from all sin" (1 John 1:7). These words describe the life to which you are called. It is a life lived in openness and honesty, a life shared with others through fellowship, and a life of purity through the blood of Jesus Christ. Herein rests the unity of the church.

Paul described this unity: "There should be no division in the body, but that the members should have the same care for one another" (1 Corinthians 12:25). In this relationship when one suffers, everyone suffers. When one rejoices, everyone rejoices. When one is honored, all share in that honor. This is the life of the church!

13   *Outward in Evangelism*

The mission of the Church was outlined by Christ:

Go therefore and make disciples of all the nations, baptizing them in the name of the Father and the Son and the Holy Spirit, teaching them to observe all that I commanded you; and lo, I am with you always, even to the end of the age (Matthew 28:19, 20).

This is the mandate of the Church.

The Assemblies of God was brought into existence to help fulfill this Great Commission. Groups of Spirit-filled believers united to reach the world for Christ. They covenanted together to make evangelism a priority. The result is today there are Assemblies of God churches around the globe. The Great Commisssion of Jesus is being fulfilled.

Your church will have a heart for world evangelization. Missionaries will be invited to share their vision and burden. You will be given the opportunity to share in world missions through giving and prayer. This will be a dynamic and thrilling part of your life in the church.

Just a caution here. Missions begins across the street and reaches from there around the world. The word *go* in the Great Commission could be translated "after you have gone." In other words, Jesus calls every believer to evangelize the world that is next to him—whether that world is America or Indonesia.

Following are some of the fundamental principles that support the world-missions thrust of the Assemblies of God.

World Evangelization Is the Commission of the Church

We believe people without Christ are lost. And only the church, empowered by the Holy Spirit, has the message of salvation. The church is under direction to bring this gospel to the lost.

Called Men and Women Are the Backbone of God's Plan to Win the World for Christ

The heathen hear the gospel preached and see it lived out through the missionary. Missionaries are sent for a given period of time, often 4 years, and then return for furlough. They live among the people to whom they have been called.

National Leaders Must Be Trained and Equipped to Build the Church

The church then becomes permanent and self-sustaining. If a country closes to foreigners, which is sometimes the case, the work of the church continues. It has its own leadership.

The Local Church Is Entrusted With the Privilege of Sending Those Who Are Called to Their Field of Service

The apostle Paul asked some appropriate questions:

How then shall they call upon Him in whom they have not believed? And how shall they believe in Him whom they have not heard? And how shall they hear without a preacher? And how shall they preach unless they are sent? (Romans 10:14, 15).

It will be joy for you to share in the sending process. Your pastor will explain to you the program for missionary support that is workable for your particular fellowship.

Prayer Is the Key to World Evangelization

A missionary may be trained, equipped, and sent. But unless his ministry on the field is supported with prayer, his effectiveness will be proportionately diminished. You must share in the work of your missionaries through prayer. They depend on you. On that great day the local church will rejoice with the worldwide Church in the victory of a shared ministry to evangelize the world. Intercessory prayer links you with the entire world and makes you a vital part of world evangelization.

Here are a few appropriate expressions of prayer as you intercede for the evangelization of the world:

—That the Word would have an open door into the hearts of men (Colossians 4:3).

—That those who minister may do so with clarity (Colossians 4:4).

—That the forces of darkness may be driven back by the power of the Holy Spirit (Ephesians 6:12).

—That the Lord would build His church around the world (Matthew 16:18).

—That those who suffer for the name of Christ may know the triumph of His cross (Matthew 5:10-12).

—That the gospel may be preached to the ends of the earth (Matthew 24:14).

Perhaps the Lord is dealing with you to become an intercessor. You will be involved in a creative, fruitful, stimulating, and inspiring ministry. You will be affecting the destiny of nations. You will be building churches in other lands. You will be sharing in the salvation of the lost around the world. You will be destroying the work of Satan and hastening the coming of the kingdom of our Lord.

What has been said about missions in this chapter is meant only to introduce you to this part of the dynamic life of the church. There is, of course, so much more. Seek to be involved in all the outreach activities—at home and abroad—that your assembly has.

Part 5

Your Church
Membership Opportunities

14   Principles for Christian Service

"When do I start?" That is the first question often asked by a zealous worker.

But wait! Has the Lord spoken to you about assuming that responsibility? Have you received the necessary training to be sure you are adequately equipped to handle the task? Has God gifted you for this particular service? These are questions that call for answers whenever you consider the work of the Lord.

Here are fundamental principles that relate to Christian service.

A Worshiping Heart

Service unto the Lord flows out of a worshiping heart. Every task of the Kingdom must be done in a context of worship. If you teach, do so in worship unto the Lord. When you give, do so as an act of worship to the Lord. When you participate in an act of mercy, do so in worship unto the Lord.

This is what I see in the life of Jesus. All the Lord did was for the glory of His Father. "Father, the hour has come; glorify Thy Son, that the Son may glorify Thee. . . . I glorified Thee on the earth, having accomplished the work which Thou hast given Me to do" (John 17:1, 4).

This is the way of satisfaction in His service. You will never tire and lose interest in your ministry when all is done as an act of worship to the Lord. You will feel perpetual refreshment in your spirit. Your heart will be made glad, and you will enjoy the flow of fellowship that comes through worship. This is the starting place for Christian service.

It is good to open each day with the prayer that the entire day will be lived as one great act of worship unto the Lord. Disappointments, failures, achievements, successes—all may be done in His name as an ascription of praise and worship unto the Lord.

You will find this principle, when lived, will bring you to new places of ministry unto the Lord and to the people who comprise your world. It is an exciting way to live!

Rooted in God's Grace

Service unto the Lord is rooted in the grace of God. The apostle Paul, reflecting on his ministry to the church at Corinth, said:

> And my message and my preaching were not in persuasive words of wisdom, but in demonstration of the Spirit and of power, that your faith should not rest on the wisdom of men, but on the power of God" (1 Corinthians 2:4, 5).

Paul understood the motivational power behind his ministry was the favor of God passing through his life. On another occasion Paul stated he was what he was simply by the grace of God (1 Corinthians 15:10).

Your achievements in the Lord's work will be measured according to God's mighty power at work within you. By the Holy Spirit your abilities and talents will be heightened to levels of achievement you could never imagine! That is His promise. He will do "exceedingly abundantly beyond all that we ask or think, according to the power that works within us" (Ephesians 3:20). This provision grows out of His amazing grace.

If this truth remains the focus of your service to the Lord and His church, you will never be disappointed. You will stand back to marvel at what the Lord by His Spirit is doing through you. All by His grace.

For God's Glory

Service for the Lord is always for the glory of the Lord. Your service to Him is never to exalt yourself. The praise that is given will be directed to the Lord. All praise will be centered in Christ.

Unfortunately the church is not always blessed with such high levels of maturity. Some believers serve to be seen and praised of men. When such praise is either absent or directed to others, they feel offended. Without continual encouragement they falter in their task. This attitude misses the goal of all service—the exaltation of Jesus Christ.

As you put your shoulder to the wheel in the local church, never lose sight of this principle. Whatever you do, do all for the glory of Christ and the building of Christ's kingdom. You will never grow weary in well-doing when guided by this principle. It will matter little to you whether your work is acclaimed by others or merely accepted with silent appreciation—for all you do is for Christ's glory alone.

By Divine Leading

Service unto the Lord is by divine leading. Where does the Lord want me? What is His direction in my life at this point? What is He speaking to my heart about areas of service unto Him?

Yes, you can know the voice of the Lord. You can determine God's will for your life relative to service. It is possible to know you are where God wants you, doing what He wants you to do. You need not settle for less.

This is an essential principle as you pray about your response to a request for your participation in an area of ministry within the church. One pastor insisted any prospective worker should make his decision on the basis of God's specific leading: "Don't say yes unless God says yes, and don't say no unless God says no."

This kind of direction is attainable—it just takes prayer and obedience. Nothing else will do if God's work is to be consistent with God's plan.

More Being Than Doing

Service unto the Lord is more through *being* than in doing. On the surface this seems contradictory. Yet this is exactly how God sees it. Moses was first a man of God—meek, faithful, and wise. Out of his walk with God came a life of dynamic service. The same can be said of Gideon, David, Daniel, and Paul. These men knew God and walked in obedience with Him. Out of their walk with God, service for God found its authority. The same is true with us.

The Lord whom we serve is more concerned about what we *are* on the inside than what we do on the outside. Only when outward activity flows out of inward power is the kingdom of God built in the hearts of men.

The prophets of long ago understood this with profound perceptibility: "This is the word of the Lord to Zerubbabel saying, 'Not by might nor by power, but by My Spirit, says the Lord of hosts' " (Zechariah 4:6).

Consider carefully your use of time, energy, and talent in the service of the Lord. Be satisfied with nothing less than a clear witness of the Holy Spirit that you are doing that which is His highest good for you. When your service for the Lord is consistent with this principle, you will avoid the weariness, discouragement, and frustration that inevitably come with any other approach to God's work.

You will want to seek the counsel of your pastor in determining areas of ministry consistent with your spiritual gifts and God-given abilities. He will be happy to discuss with you your specific place in the body of Christ.

A Spirit-Controlled Temperament

Service unto the Lord demands a Spirit-controlled temperament. You might as well face it now: the church is not a paradise, nor is it a place where perfect people are found. You will meet some in the church whom you simply do not like. They will rub you the wrong way. Personality conflicts, impatient attitudes, selfishness, greed—you'll meet them all in the church.

Objection? "I thought the church was the bride of Christ, pure and spotless. How can these other things exist?"

The church, like the believer, stands complete only in Jesus Christ. Perfection is in Him, by His grace, and will be fully satisfied only at His coming.

It is in this context you are asked to serve. Every relationship, whether deemed good or bad, will be an opportunity for spiritual growth and blessing. It will all depend on your attitude and spirit. The church provides the garden in which the fruit of the Spirit is to grow. And your heart will be its soil.

15   Gifts for Service

The Holy Spirit has equipped the Church to do its work in the world. Each member has been given the necessary gifts of enablement to fulfill God's call on his life.

Now there are varieties of gifts, but the same Spirit. And there are varieties of ministries, and the same Lord. And there are varieties of effects, but the same God who works all things in all persons (1 Corinthians 12:4-6).

The task before the Church is the recognition, development, and release of these gifts. This is the key to the dynamic of the Church in the world.

A brief outline and summary of all the spiritual gifts will be given here, with further emphasis and detail given to the ministry gifts.

The Gifts of the Spirit

Power Gifts	*Revelational Gifts*	*Vocal Gifts*
Healing	Wisdom	Prophecy
Miracles	Knowledge	Unknown Tongues
Faith	Discerning of Spirits	Interpretation of Unknown Tongues

The Gifts of Calling

The Holy Spirit has called certain members of the Body for specific ministry (Ephesians 4:11; 1 Corinthians 12:28).

1. Apostles. One who is called and enabled to go out from the local body to establish churches in other places.

2. Prophets. One who is called and enabled to speak the Word of God to the church with unction, power, and authority.

3. Evangelists. One who is called and enabled to announce the good news of the gospel to those who are lost.

4. Shepherds and teachers. One who is called and enabled to tend and teach the flock of God.

5. Workers of miracles. One who is called and enabled to perform the miraculous by God's specially given power.

6. Ministry of healing. One who is called and enabled to heal the sick by God's specially given power.

7. Helps. One who is called and enabled to perform helpful deeds in ministering to the body of Christ.

8. Administration. One who is called and enabled to administer, organize, and govern the activities and work of the church.

The Ministry Gifts

"As each one has received a special gift, employ it in serving one another, as good stewards of the manifold grace of God" (1 Peter 4:10).

The ministry gifts (Romans 12:6-8) provide the fundamental and basic equipment of the church to minister to itself and to its world. If these gifts are in operation, the church will have a full and complete ministry. Their absence will mark the demise of the church—both to its identity as an instrument of God in this world and as an agent of healing and blessing to a needy and lost people.

1. Prophecy. This gift provides the enablement to speak forth the Word of the Lord to the church with unction, authority, and power. It is distinguished from the "vocal" gift of prophecy and the "calling" gift of prophecy, only in that it is more general in its meaning. It has to do with motivation for practical service to the body of Christ.

It is not, therefore, restricted to specific times when the body has gathered for worship (vocal gift of prophecy), nor to the specific office which one may hold in the body (calling gift of prophecy). It refers to the work of the Holy Spirit in the believer's life to enable him to practically and positively apply the Word of the Lord to the particular circumstances of people.

Individuals possessing this gift will seek opportunities to give the word they feel they have received from the Lord. Believers so gifted will be able to discern between good and evil. They will be direct, eager, persuasive, and frank. They will hate sin, be quick to correct, and very sensitive to God's view on any subject.

Brokenness and weeping will evidence their deep concern for the spiritual health of God's people. Though often misunderstood and criticized, they will persist in faithfully discharging the Word of the Lord.

Believers who have received this gift of ministry will need to guard against pride, control, harshness, judgmentalism, and self-righteousness. Romans 12:9 gives the guidelines for the fulfillment of the prophetic ministry: "Let love be without hypocrisy. Abhor what is evil; cling to what is good." This is a needed and blessed provision of the Spirit for the strengthening and guidance of the body of Christ.

2. *Serving.* The gift of serving provides for the believer the fundamental motivation and desire to demonstrate the love of Jesus Christ by ministering to the practical needs of people. It is the ability first to see the needs of people and then to respond appropriately to those needs.

Martha possessed this gift when she ministered to the needs of Jesus. Dorcas and a host of others blessed the church by reaching out to people in need.

The members of the body who have been blessed with this gift are easily recognized. They are quick to volunteer when help is needed. They have an inherent ability to sense the needs of others. Somehow they know just the right thing to do at just the right time to meet critical needs in the lives of others. As long as they know a need exists, you can count on their positive and helpful response.

Believers with this gift may appear to be overzealous, insensitive to what others may be doing, and imbalanced with physical rather than spiritual concerns. They may sometimes be so anxious to help that they get in the way of what others are seeking to do. The concern for meeting an immediate need may blind them from seeing the overall work God may be doing in a life. There may be a tendency to become "ego-dependent" on the compliments and approvals that are generated by acts of kindness.

Romans 12:10 is the directive for the proper use of this beautiful gift: "Be devoted to one another in brotherly love; give preference to one another in honor."

Or consider the practical admonition of James:

104

If a brother or sister is without clothing and in need of daily food, and one of you says to them, "Go in peace, be warmed and be filled," and yet you do not give them what is necessary for their body, what use is that? (James 2:15, 16).

That puts the accent where it belongs and establishes the necessity for this gift of ministry to flourish in the church.

3. *Teaching.* The gift of teaching provides the believer with the motivation to seek for truth and then to present that truth to others. This gift is clearly illustrated in the life and ministry of Apollos:

Now a certain Jew named Apollos, an Alexandrian by birth, an eloquent man, came to Ephesus; and he was mighty in the Scriptures. This man had been instructed in the way of the Lord; and being fervent in spirit, he was speaking and teaching accurately the things concerning Jesus (Acts 18:24, 25).

The text goes on to explain that when Priscilla and Aquila, who also possessed the gift of teaching, heard Apollos, "they took him aside and explained to him the way of God more accurately" (v. 26). Having received this instruction, Apollos "helped greatly those who had believed through grace; for he powerfully refuted the Jews in public, demonstrating by the Scriptures that Jesus was the Christ" (vv. 27, 28).

The gift of teaching is easily recognized. Believers possessing this gift find delight in research, have a profound interest in the meanings of words, are systematic in their analysis and presentation of the truth, have an abhorrence for careless speculations, and are never satisfied until both sides of an issue have been carefully explored. They are quick to argue for the necessity of this particular gift and its fundamental importance in purifying the body of Jesus Christ from error and misunderstanding.

The gift falls into misuse when those who claim it put theory over practice and relegate human need to a place of secondary importance. The quest for truth, valid and essential, must always keep the preeminent ministry of the Holy Spirit in focus—for it is the specific work of the Spirit to reveal truth to the human heart. Human intellect and precise research can never equal or match the ministry of the Holy Spirit.

There is also the danger that those who possess the gift may become preoccupied with the minutia of the Word and fail to relate the parts to the whole. As we have seen with the other gifts, the element of pride can easily creep in if proper perspective is not maintained.

The apostle Paul provided the guidelines for the proper use of the gift of teaching: "Be diligent to present yourself approved to God as a workman who does not need to be ashamed, handling accurately the word of truth" (2 Timothy 2:15). And James added: "Let not many of you become teachers, my brethren, knowing that as such we shall incur a stricter judgment" (James 3:1).

This is a blessed and essential gift. It is the faithful discharge of this particular gift that makes the church strong in the knowledge of God and His Word. Men and women, called of God to teach, lay in human hearts a foundation of spiritual truth on which well-ordered and productive lives may be built. The heart of the teacher is described in Romans 12:11: "'Not lagging behind in diligence, fervent in spirit, serving the Lord."

4. Exhortation. Believers who possess the gift of exhortation (encouragement) will be enabled to stimulate and build the faith of others.

A clear example of this gift is found in the life and ministry of Barnabas, whose name appropriately means "Son of Encouragement" (Acts 4:36):

But Barnabas took hold of him and brought him to the apostles and described to them how he had seen the Lord on the road, and that He had talked to him, and how at Damascus he had spoken out boldly in the name of Jesus (Acts 9:27).

The body of Christ is profoundly blessed by those who have received the gift of exhortation. They are "faith builders." They have an eye for the good and the positive. They see and commend strong points of character in others. They see God's mighty power at work even in the tragedies and misfortunes of life.

The practical aspects of life concern them most, and they seek for opportunities to demonstrate their faith. This gift provides the "lubricant" to keep the church motivated and encouraged to fulfill its call.

Those who possess this gift need to guard against oversimplification, overconfidence, and half-truths. Misuse here can lead to a kind of humanism that views faith more in terms of personal attitude than as a revelation of divine truth. An unrealistic and shallow understanding of human need can manifest itself if this gift is not kept in proper perspective.

The church, however, needs to see the profound importance of this gift to the body of Christ. At every turn there needs to be someone who can rise to the occasion and declare that God is at work in spite of circumstances and that spiritual victory is inevitable as long as faith in God is held in honor. The spirit of this gift is illustrated in Romans 12:12: "Rejoicing in hope, persevering in tribulation, devoted to prayer."

5. *Giving.* The gift of giving has to do with the en-

ablement and motivation to be generous in sharing what we have with others. The Scriptures are adequately illustrative: Malachi taught the people to support the house of God with tithes and offerings; the widow gave all she had to the temple treasury: and the Good Samaritan gave his time, his provisions, and his money to rescue the man who had fallen into the hands of robbers.

Believers who are gifted to give have a special ability to handle money. They make wise investments, are able to assess a need as to its validity and propriety, and able to motivate others to join them in giving. They are people of faith. They see giving as a consequence of their partnership with God.

Although some have been granted the specific gift of giving, every believer is to share in the joy of giving. Included here are several principles for giving that will be helpful to you:

a. Giving involves more than money. Everything that is ours belongs to God. We are but stewards of His gifts. This means God has first claim on our time, our talents, our possessions, and our total resources.

b. The tithe is the Lord's. The prophet Malachi set the pattern: "You are cursed with a curse, for you are robbing Me, the whole nation of you! Bring the whole tithe into the storehouse" (Malachi 3:9, 10).

One point does need to be reemphasized. Under grace the motivation for giving is love. The believer gives with joy, gratitude, and deep devotion. Gifts are given as an act of worship to the Lord. The legalistic requirements of the Law have passed, and in their place has come the motivational power of love.

c. The tithe belongs in the storehouse. Ten percent of

the believer's earnings should be given for the support of the local church to carry out its ministry.

According to Malachi, it is the tithe especially that is to be placed in the storehouse. Offerings do not appear to be included in the directive. We may assume then that the offering may be used to support the work of the Lord wherever God may so direct.

d. Mix faith with your gift. God has promised to bless faithfulness in giving. "Giving to get" is obviously a low level of motivation for giving. Yet God does bless those who are faithful in giving. The believer does not give out of duty and requirement but out of obedience and love. And the consequence of properly motivated giving will be God's blessings.

6. *Administration.* The believer who has been granted the gift of administration will possess the ability to organize properly the work of the body of Christ. Talents will be matched with tasks, workers will be motivated to serve, and God's work will go forward. No church can fulfill its mission without the presence of individuals so gifted.

It is not hard to spot the members of the body who are called to lead. They have an eye for what needs to be done. They can immediately evaluate the options for accomplishing the task. They seem to know "just the one" who can get the job done.

This gift of ministry, like the others, will sometimes be misunderstood. Some may feel they are being pushed and feel a degree of resentment. Others may react with jealousy, wondering why they cannot be in a place of leadership. A certain amount of controversy inevitably gathers around those who lead. They are the ones who must make decisions and give directions—and some will level criticism whenever disagreements arise.

The body of Christ cannot move on without the presence and practice of this spiritual gift. If God has so gifted you, be courageous and obedient. After the criticism is past and the controversy is over, you will be able to see a beautiful work that God has done through you. It is worth it if you are called to lead.

A word of caution: Seek to know and follow the will of the Lord. Practice the presence and spirit of Jesus. If you do, those who follow will be enriched and blessed, and the body of Christ will move on in unity and power.

7. *Mercy.* The Lord has provided full care and ministry to His body. To assure completeness, the Holy Spirit has gifted certain members with the ability to identify with and comfort those who are in distress. It is that unusual ability to sense hurt and to recognize grief—to empathize and relate.

The Good Samaritan is a classic example of this gift in operation. The religious elite passed by on the other side of the road without being moved with compassion. Not so the Samaritan. He put himself next to the man in need and did what was necessary to bring the man back to health.

What are the characteristics of those believers who possess the ministry gift of showing mercy? They are sensitive to feelings and emotions of people. They understand the significance of voice inflections, moods, and attitudes. They are benevolent, compassionate, accepting, and caring.

When a fellow believer comes up to share his concern for your needs, you may wonder how he knew and how his words could have been so appropriately chosen. Well, now you know. That person has been gifted of the Holy Spirit to minister mercy to you in a time of need.

If this is your gift, there may be some who will misunderstand. They will feel you are guided by intuition, you are trying to push yourself on others, or you are too emotional about life in general.

It is impossible to avoid misunderstanding in any area of ministry. All the Lord expects of any of us is obedience. Listen for divine direction, keep a check on your own motivation, and then be satisfied that the Lord will bring to birth the plan He has for your life and the lives of others whom you serve.

Your Place

The major cause for church division and disunity is the failure to recognize and honor the ministry gifts. Those gifted to teach may resent those gifted to administer. Those who are gifted to show mercy may feel those gifted with prophecy are harsh and unsympathetic. You are called to practice in obedience the gift or gifts God has given you and hold in honor the other members of the body who are gifted differently than you.

Paul said all these gifts have been granted for one reason: "For the equipping of the saints for the work of service, to the building up of the body of Christ" (Ephesians 4:12). In other words, you have been endowed and gifted for one reason—to build up the body of Christ. It is time now to do just that!

I have a recommendation. Make an appointment to see your pastor. Discuss with him your place in the body and ask him for prayer and guidance in the discovering and maturing of the ministry gift that has been given to you. You will find the Holy Spirit will anoint the abilities and talents you possess and focus them into one or more of the ministry areas outlined above. What you have thought to be a "natural endowment" by the

Creator will now, by the power of the Holy Spirit, become a "divine endowment" to fulfill the ministry God has for you.

Not only will you want to discover your ministry gift and use it freely, but you will also want to help others understand and discover theirs as well. This is both your place of privilege and responsibility in the body of Christ. Do not miss either. Your brother and sister are like you—waiting to be used to bless and build the kingdom of God. Why not share freely—for in blessing you will be blessed, and in giving you will receive.

This is the key to service unto the Lord in the church. Each member discovers his special gift of ministry and develops it into ministry in a context of commitment and loyalty. The body of Christ is then well furnished in every way. Recruiting workers is no problem—for already there are members called to do the task. As they serve, it is not to accommodate others; it is to obey the call of Christ on their lives.

When the gifts and ministries of the Holy Spirit are functioning properly in the body of Christ, the church is vibrant and strong. Every facet of its ministry is complete. The vision is realized. The plan is accomplished.

You are in the very center of this triumphant event. For you are the church! "As each one has received a spiritual gift, employ it in serving one another, as good stewards of the manifold grace of God" (1 Peter 4:10).

Part 6

Your Home
and Its Christian Influence

16   The Family and the Church

"Dad, who made God?"

"How long is forever?"

Simple questions that demand profound answers!

Children—they have little minds that know how to ask big questions. But it is a necessary part of the growing process, that mysterious journey from infancy to adulthood.

Who is going to answer? What is the climate that will foster growth? Where do children learn where they fit in a big world?

God has ordained the family for such a purpose. A place of love, acceptance, joy, and fun. A place where no one feels alone—and any question counts. There is no other place like this in all the world.

That is what this chapter is all about—the family! And not just the family, but the family and the church—both working together to bring the love of God and His grace into life itself.

God himself created the family when He made Adam and Eve. He placed them in a perfect environment where they could live and grow. God said; "They shall become one flesh" (Genesis 2:24).

From then until now God's plan has included the

family. Even the fall into sin did not destroy the relationship that God intended through the family.

What is the family? The answer is found in Genesis 2:24: "For this cause a man shall leave his father and his mother, and shall cleave to his wife." Whenever this happens, a family is born. A man and woman leave the family to which they have been attached, and together they form a new social unit which is called the family. It is God's idea—and that is why the family will always be.

Jesus made it clear that from the beginning God had ordained the family:

"Is it lawful for a man to divorce his wife for any cause at all?" And He answered and said, "Have you not read, that He who created them from the beginning made them male and female, . . . they are no more two, but one flesh [speaking of marriage]. What therefore God has joined together, let no man separate" (Matthew 19:3, 4, 6).

Jesus went on to explain to the inquiring Pharisees that Moses' bill of divorcement in no way changed God's original plan. That provision in the Law for divorce came about only because of the hardness of men's hearts.

It is interesting too that Jesus chose to perform His first miracle at a wedding (John 2). By His presence He blessed and sanctified that particular wedding and in a sense the very institution we call marriage. Whenever the Lord taught about the subject of marriage, it was with the highest regard and the deepest respect. Jesus understood the importance of strong families.

The loving church dedicates itself to help families grow stronger, and it does not condemn those who have experienced unfortunate marital problems. This is a time the loving church demonstrates love, concern, and healing toward those who have gone through the trauma of divorce.

What makes a marriage strong? There are three affinities that are imperative.

First, a marriage must find a *mental affinity*. Husband and wife must share the world of ideas with one another. They must maintain open lines of meaningful communication—finding mutual strength through the exchange of ideas.

Second, a marriage must find a *physical affinity*. Sexual love has fallen into abuse in the world. Lust, not love, characterizes much of what the world says about marriage. God intended, however, that sexual love should be an expression of deepest joy and heartfelt emotion. When sexual love is enjoyed within the parameters of marriage, God is honored; He made it to be that way.

Third, a marriage must find a *spiritual affinity*. God must be the center of any marriage that is totally fulfilling. Prayer, worship, and the study of God's Word are essential ingredients for any successful and happy marriage.

What does it mean then to "leave and cleave"? It means (1) a physical separation from parents, (2) a psychological separation from parents, and (3) an economic separation from parents. Not that parents are no longer needed or desired, but simply that marriage presupposes the function of a new social unit. Old ties need to be broken so new ones may be developed.

Marriage, therefore, is a private relationship. It involves trust. No other person has right of entry—not even parents.

Trust is the greatest treasure of marriage. To cultivate

and preserve trust is the highest priority of marriage. Without it the relationship cannot exist as God intended.

The church plays such a vital role in building strong marriage relationships. The teaching of God's Word, the fellowship God's people, and the involvement in the work of the Lord have a strengthening effect on the marriage relationship. Couples who actively seek the Lord and the fellowship of the church will be strong in their commitment to one another. Christ in the center of the marriage will bring to that relationship a quality of life and experience that will be rich and compensating.

Roles Within the Family

Consider the order God has established for the family.

1. The Role of the father. Job was a priest in his home. It was his custom to rise early in the morning and offer burnt offerings unto the Lord on behalf of each of his children: "Perhaps my sons have sinned and cursed God in their hearts" (Job 1:5). He stood between God and his family to bring their needs to God and to invoke on them the blessing of God.

It is the duty and privilege of the father to be the priest in his own home. As such, he is entrusted with the responsibility of teaching the Scriptures by word and example, directing the family in prayer, and leading his family in the ways of righteousness. His leadership carries with it an authority that brings order to his family.

God has placed him as the head of his family. In love, sacrifice, and self-denial he imparts life and truth. Through him the blessings of the Lord are made rich to the entire family.

2. The Role of the mother. To her is granted the privilege and duty of raising the children and working with her husband as together they direct the affairs of the family.

She is usually the primary influence with the children. She cares for them from infancy and has a God-given ability to teach her children the ways of God.

It is also the privilege of the wife to pray for and support her husband as he faces the task of providing for his family. The harshness of the world loses its sting when a wife shows her love and support for her husband.

The wife too deserves the support of her husband in her responsibilities as well. It boils down to a life of sharing and cooperation—each trying to outdo the other in sharing love and practicing patience.

3. *The Role of children.* One commandment carries with it a promise: "Honor your father and your mother, that your days may be prolonged in the land which the Lord your God gives you" (Exodus 20:12). By this God shows how important it is in His sight that children honor their parents. Based on this honor, a child develops the proper regard for God, for society, and for himself.

But how is this honor cultivated? Discipline with love, instruction from the Scriptures, and exemplary Christian conduct provide the means by which a child may develop an attitude of parental honor and respect.

Principles for Family Solidarity

Listed here are basic guidelines that will produce strong family units.

1. *An understanding of God and His ways must be taught.* Deuteronomy 6 provides the pattern. The Word becomes the final authority for the home. Thinking,

conduct, and attitude are all measured by the Scriptures.

2. An attitude of trust must be communicated. A teenage son, for example, will be challenged by a demonstration of trust: "Son, I have confidence that you are able to make a proper decision in this matter."

Trust will encourage maturity and provide an opportunity for good decisionmaking. Well-chosen compliments, expressions of love and appreciation, and sympathetic listening will do much to strengthen the family. It starts with trust.

3. A family altar must be built. Busy and irregular schedules militate against a regular time for family worship. You will need to be persistent in insisting the members of the family gather regularly for this important activity. It is true the family that prays together stays together.

"How do I go about conducting family worship in my home?" Here are a few suggestions:

a. Have each member of the family contribute something to the worship time—a song, a verse, a game, a testimony, or a prayer.

b. Discuss as a family the practical implications of the passage of Scripture that has been read. "John, how does this truth relate to the problem you are now having with math?"

c. Provide an opportunity during family worship for the members of the family to share some of the concerns and needs they feel as part of the family. "Dad, I am beginning to feel like you aren't really listening to us when we come to you with a problem." Family worship time provides the occasion to air such feelings and then make them a matter of prayer.

d. Discover new things to do during the worship

time. You may wish to go on a hike, visit a place of historic importance, or do an act of kindness for a neighbor as a part of your worship together as a family. Many spiritual lessons can be taught through selected activities.

4. Time to be together must be a priority. There is no substitute for being together as a family. Do not allow your schedule to rob you of the needed time to be with your family. It may be necessary to set aside times just for the family. A particular night each week may be helpful. But be careful that family time is not made to compete with every other demand. The family has first claim.

5. The family must share in the life of the church. This is why this chapter has a place in a book on church membership. The home and the church cannot be separated. They are parts of the same composite. The life of the home cannot be separated from the life of the church. The church and the home share a common purpose. They both teach the Scriptures, demonstrate a way of life that is consistent with the Word, and provide an atmosphere of acceptance and love.

You will be blessing your family by being sure each member is an integral part of the life of the church. It is your responsibility to see this happens. The church will work with you, but it is your responsibility to train your child in the importance of being a part of the body of Christ.

Some have tried to transfer that responsibility to the church, but it simply does not work. The home is still the primary influence in the spiritual development of a child. The church is there to assist and help, but the spiritual thrust of the home is still the key.

Singles

The Scriptures teach by example and precept that not everyone is called to be part of an individual family. Some members of the body of Christ are called to serve the Lord as singles. They are free from many of the normal responsibilities that go with family life and are free to devote themselves more fully to the work of the Lord. Singles are of great value in the body of Christ. They have a special place to fill.

If you are single and you know you are in the will of God, be excited about the place of ministry to which God has called you. You are not in a secondary position—it really is not a couples' world. We are all members together of the family of God. Every believer is a member of this family.

Special Ministries of the Church

In a variety of ways the church reaches out to families in service and ministry.

The church is there to provide counsel, facilities, and direction for weddings.

It is prepared to assist parents as they dedicate their children to the Lord.

When a death has occurred, the church is there to share the sorrow and to support the family with its love and encouragement as well as assist in the funeral arrangements and memorial service.

Whenever you have a need, you can turn to the church. It is the nature of the church to care.

Naturally customs will vary from place to place and from church to church regarding these special ministries of the church. Some pastors, for example, require several counseling sessions with the prospective bride and groom to stress principles for building a strong foundation for a Christian home.

But in times of test and trial, most church members turn first to their pastor and then to other members of their assembly for comfort, strength, counsel, and prayer. It's a way of growing together.

By acting together the church can provide sustenance for members and for others hit by misfortune and disaster.

The list could go on and on. In so many ways the local church exists to serve you and your family—and to provide you with the thrilling, growing experience of serving, helping, maturing, and being all the Lord intends you to be.

Your church needs you; you need your church. But remember: Church membership is not merely signing your name to a membership card. What really counts is the commitment that signature represents.

If you haven't already done so, call your pastor right now. Tell him you want to identify with this local church, to be a part of this growing-together process. And be prepared to grow in God's grace!

Appendix

Statement of Fundamental Truths

The Bible is our all-sufficient rule for faith and practice. This Statement of Fundamental Truths is intended simply as a basis of fellowship among us (i.e., that we all speak the same thing, 1 Cor. 1:10; Acts 2:42). The phraseology employed in this Statement is not inspired or contended for, but the truth set forth is held to be essential to a Full-Gospel ministry. No claim is made that it contains all Biblical truth, only that it covers our need as to these fundamental doctrines.

1. The Scriptures Inspired

The Scriptures, both the Old and New Testaments, are verbally inspired of God and are the revelation of God to man, the infallible, authoritative rule of faith and conduct (2 Tim. 3:15-17; 1 Thess. 2:13; 2 Peter 1:21).

2. The One True God

The one true God has revealed himself as the eternally self-existent "I AM," the Creator of heaven and earth and the Redeemer of mankind. He has further revealed himself as embodying the principles of relationship and association as Father, Son, and Holy Ghost (Deut. 6:4; Isaiah 43:10,11; Matt. 28:19; Luke 3:22).

THE ADORABLE GODHEAD

(a) Terms Defined
The terms "Trinity" and "persons," as related to the Godhead, while not found in the Scriptures, are words in harmony with Scripture, whereby we may convey to others our immediate understanding of the doctrine of Christ respecting the Being of God, as distinguished from "gods many and lords many." We therefore may speak with propriety of the Lord our God, who is One Lord, as a trinity or as one Being of three persons, and still be absolutely scriptural (examples, Matt. 28:19; 2 Cor. 13:14; John 14:16,17).
(b) Distinction and Relationship in the Godhead
Christ taught a distinction of Persons in the Godhead which He expressed in specific terms of relationship, as Father, Son, and Holy Ghost, but that this distinction and relationship, as to its mode is inscrutable and incomprehensible, because unexplained. Luke 1:35; 1 Cor. 1:24; Matt. 11:25-27; 28:19; 2 Cor. 13:14; 1 John 1:3,4.
(c) Unity of the One Being of Father, Son, and Holy Ghost
Accordingly, therefore, there is that in the Son which constitutes Him **the Son and** not the Father; and there is **that** in the Holy Ghost which constitutes Him **the Holy Ghost** and not either the Father or the Son.

124

Wherefore the Father is the Begetter, the Son is the Begotten; and the Holy Ghost is the One proceeding from the Father and the Son. Therefore, because these three persons in the Godhead are in a state of unity, there is but one Lord God Almighty and His name one. John 1:18; 15:26; 17:11,21; Zech. 14:9.

(d) Identity and Cooperation in the Godhead

The Father, the Son, and the Holy Ghost are never identical as to Person; nor confused as to relation; nor divided in respect to the Godhead; nor opposed as to cooperation. The Son is in the Father and the Father is in the Son as to relationship. The Son is with the Father and the Father is with the Son, as to fellowship. The Father is not from the Son, but the Son is from the Father, as to authority. The Holy Ghost is from the Father and the Son proceeding, as to nature, relationship, cooperation and authority. Hence neither Person in the Godhead either exists or works separately or independently of the others. John 5:17-30,32,37; John 8:17,18.

(e) The Title, Lord Jesus Christ

The appellation, "Lord Jesus Christ," is a proper name. It is never applied, in the New Testament, either to the Father or to the Holy Ghost. It therefore belongs exclusively to the Son of God. Rom. 1:1-3,7; 2 John 3.

(f) The Lord Jesus Christ, God with us

The Lord Jesus Christ, as to His divine and eternal nature, is the proper and only Begotten of the Father, but as to His human nature, He is the proper Son of Man. He is, therefore, acknowledged to be both God and man; who because He is God and man, is "Immanuel," God with us. Matt. 1:23; 1 John 4:2,10,14; Rev. 1:13,17.

(g) The Title, Son of God

Since the name "Immanuel" embraces both God and man in the one Person, our Lord Jesus Christ, it follows that the title, Son of God, describes His proper deity, and the title Son of Man, His proper humanity. Therefore, the title, Son of God, belongs to the order of eternity, and the title, Son of Man to the order of time. Matt. 1:21-23; 2 John 3; 1 John 3:8; Heb. 7:3; 1:1-13.

(h) Transgression of the Doctrine of Christ

Wherefore, it is a transgression of the Doctrine of Christ to say that Jesus Christ derived the title, Son of God, solely from the fact of the incarnation, or because of His relation to the economy of redemption. Therefore, to deny that the Father is a real and eternal Father, and that the Son is a real and eternal Son, is a denial of the distinction and relationship in the Being of God; a denial of the Father and the Son; and a displacement of the truth that Jesus Christ is come in the flesh. 2 John 9; John 1:1,2,14,18,29,49; 1 John 2:22,23; 4:1-5; Heb. 12:2.

(i) Exaltation of Jesus Christ as Lord

The Son of God, our Lord Jesus Christ, having by himself purged our sins, sat down on the right hand of the Majesty on high; angels and principalities and powers having been made subject unto Him. And having been made both Lord and Christ, He sent the Holy Ghost that we, in the name of Jesus, might bow our knees and confess that Jesus Christ is Lord to the glory of God the Father until the end, when the Son shall become subject to the Father that God may be all in all. Heb. 1:3; 1 Peter 2:9; Acts 2:32-36; Rom. 14:11; 1 Cor. 15:24-28.

(j) Equal Honor to the Father and to the Son

Wherefore, since the Father has delivered all judgment unto the Son, it is not only the express duty of all in heaven and on earth to bow the knee, but it is an unspeakable joy in the Holy Ghost to ascribe unto the Son all the attributes of Deity, and to give Him all the honor and the glory contained in all the names and titles of the Godhead (except those which express relationship. See paragraphs b, c, and d), and thus honor the Son even as we honor the Father. John 5:22,23; 1 Peter 1:8; Rev. 5:6-14; Phil. 2:8,9; Rev. 7:9,10; 4:8-11.

3. The Deity of the Lord Jesus Christ

The Lord Jesus Christ is the eternal Son of God. The Scriptures declare:

(a) His virgin birth (Matthew 1:23; Luke 1:31,35).

(b) His sinless life (Hebrews 7:26; 1 Peter 2:22).

(c) His miracles (Acts 2:22; 10:38).

(d) His substitutionary work on the cross (1 Cor. 15:3; 2 Cor. 5:21).

(e) His bodily resurrection from the dead (Matthew 28:6; Luke 24:39; 1 Cor. 15:4).

(f) His exaltation to the right hand of God (Acts 1:9,11; 2:33; Philippians 2:9-11; Hebrews 1-3).

4. The Fall of Man

Man was created good and upright; for God said, "Let us make man in our image, after our likeness." However, man by voluntary transgression fell and thereby incurred not only physical death but also spiritual death, which is separation from God (Genesis 1:26,27; 2:17; 3:6; Romans 5:12-19).

5. The Salvation of Man

Man's only hope of redemption is through the shed blood of Jesus Christ the Son of God.

(a) Conditions to Salvation

Salvation is received through repentance toward God and faith toward the Lord Jesus Christ. By the washing of regeneration and renewing of the Holy Ghost, being justified by grace through faith, man becomes an heir of God according to the hope of eternal life (Luke 24:47; John 3:3; Romans 10:13-15; Ephesians 2:8; Titus 2:11; 3:5-7).

(b) The Evidences of Salvation

The inward evidence of salvation is the direct witness of the Spirit (Romans 8:16). The outward evidence to all men is a life of righteousness and true holiness (Eph. 4:24; Titus 2:12).

6. The Ordinances of the Church

(a) Baptism in Water

The ordinance of baptism by immersion is commanded in the Scriptures. All who repent and believe on Christ as Saviour and Lord are to be baptized. Thus they declare to the world that they have died with Christ and that they also have been raised with Him to walk in newness of life. (Matthew 28:19; Mark 16:16; Acts 10:47,48; Romans 6:4).

(b) Holy Communion

The Lord's Supper, consisting of the elements—bread and the fruit of the vine—is the symbol expressing our sharing the divine nature of our Lord Jesus Christ (2 Peter 1:4): a memorial of His suffering and death (1 Cor. 11:26); and a prophecy of His second coming (1 Cor. 11:26); and is enjoined on all believers "till He come!"

7. The Baptism in the Holy Ghost

All believers are entitled to and should ardently expect and earnestly seek the promise of the Father, the baptism in the Holy Ghost and fire, according to the command of our Lord Jesus Christ. This was the normal experience of all in the early Christian Church. With it comes the enduement of power for life and service, the bestowment of the gifts and their uses in the work of the ministry (Luke 24:49; Acts 1:4,8; 1 Cor. 12:1-31). This experience is distinct from and subsequent to the experience of the new birth (Acts 8:12-17; 10:44-46; 11:

14-16; 15:7-9). With the baptism in the Holy Ghost come such experiences as an overflowing fullness of the Spirit (John 7:37-39; Acts 4:8), a deepened reverence for God (Acts 2:43; Heb. 12:28), an intensified consecration to God and dedication to His work (Acts 2:42), and a more active love for Christ, for His Word, and for the lost (Mark 16:20).

8. The Evidence of the Baptism in the Holy Ghost

The baptism of believers in the Holy Ghost is witnessed by the initial physical sign of speaking with other tongues as the Spirit of God gives them utterance (Acts 2:4). The speaking in tongues in this instance is the same in essence as the gift of tongues (1 Cor. 12:4-10,28), but different in purpose and use.

9. Sanctification

Sanctification is an act of separation from that which is evil, and of dedication unto God (Rom. 12:1,2; 1 Thess. 5:23; Heb. 13:12). The Scriptures teach a life of "holiness without which no man shall see the Lord" (Heb. 12:14). By the power of the Holy Ghost we are able to obey the command: "Be ye holy, for I am holy" (1 Peter 1:15,16).

Sanctification is realized in the believer by recognizing his identification with Christ in His death and resurrection, and by faith reckoning daily upon the fact of that union, and by offering every faculty continually to the dominion of the Holy Spirit (Rom. 6:1-11,13; 8:1,2,13; Gal. 2:20; Phil. 2:12,13; 1 Peter 1:5).

10. The Church and Its Mission

The Church is the Body of Christ, the habitation of God through the Spirit, with divine appointments for the fulfillment of her great commission. Each believer, born of the Spirit, is an integral part of the General Assembly and Church of the Firstborn, which are written in heaven (Ephesians 1:22,23; 2:22; Hebrews 12:23).

Since God's purpose concerning man is to seek and to save that which is lost, to be worshiped by man, and to build a body of believers in the image of His Son, the priority reason-for-being of the Assemblies of God as part of the Church is:

a. To be an agency of God for evangelizing the world (Acts 1:8; Matthew 28:19,20; Mark 16:15,16).
b. To be a corporate body in which man may worship God (1 Corinthians 12:13).
c. To be a channel of God's purpose to build a body of saints being perfected in the image of His Son (Ephesians 4:11-16; 1 Corinthians 12:28; 1 Corinthians 14:12).

The Assemblies of God exists expressly to give continuing emphasis to this reason-for-being in the New Testament apostolic pattern by teaching and encouraging believers to be baptized in the Holy Spirit. This experience:

a. Enables them to evangelize in the power of the Spirit with accompanying supernatural signs (Mark 16:15-20; Acts 4:29-31; Hebrews 2:3,4).
b. Adds a necessary dimension to worshipful relationship with God (1 Corinthians 2:10-16; 1 Corinthians 12,13, and 14).
c. Enables them to respond to the full working of the Holy Spirit in expression of fruit and gifts and ministries as

in New Testament times for the edifying of the body of Christ (Galatians 5:22-26; 1 Corinthians 14:12; Ephesians 4:11,12; 1 Corinthians 12:28; Colossians 1:29).

11. The Ministry

A divinely called and scripturally ordained ministry has been provided by our Lord for the threefold purpose of leading the Church in: (1) Evangelization of the world (Mark 16:15-20), (2) Worship of God (John 4:23,24), (3) Building a body of saints being perfected in the image of His Son (Ephesians 4:11-16).

12. Divine Healing

Divine healing is an integral part of the gospel. Deliverance from sickness is provided for in the atonement, and is the privilege of all believers (Isaiah 53:4,5; Matt. 8:16,17; James 5:14-16).

13. The Blessed Hope

The resurrection of those who have fallen asleep in Christ and their translation together with those who are alive and remain unto the coming of the Lord is the imminent and blessed hope of the church (1 Thess. 4:16,17; Romans 8:23; Titus 2:13; 1 Cor. 15:51,52).

14. The Millennial Reign of Christ

The second coming of Christ includes the rapture of the saints, which is our blessed hope, followed by the visible return of Christ with His saints to reign on the earth for one thousand years (Zech. 14:15; Matt. 24:27,30; Revelation 1:7; 19:11-14; 20:1-6). This millennial reign will bring the salvation of national Israel (Ezekiel 37:21,22; Zephaniah 3:19,20; Romans 11:26,27) and the establishment of universal peace (Isaiah 11:6-9; Psalm 72:3-8; Micah 4:3,4).

15. The Final Judgment

There will be a final judgment in which the wicked dead will be raised and judged according to their works. Whosoever is not found written in the Book of Life, together with the devil and his angels, the beast and the false prophet, will be consigned to everlasting punishment in the lake which burneth with fire and brimstone, which is the second death (Matt. 25:46; Mark 9:43-48; Revelation 19:20; 20:11-15; 21:8).

16 The New Heavens and the New Earth

"We, according to His promise, look for new heavens and a new earth wherein dwelleth righteousness" (2 Peter 3:13; Revelation 21,22).